Too Young to Get Old

CHRISTINE WEBBER

piatkus

To DGD
With all my love
Thanks for being far too young to get old

PIATKUS

First published in Great Britain in 2010 by Piatkus
Copyright © Christine Webber 2010

Cartoons copyright © Jacky Fleming 2010
www.jackyfleming.co.uk

A CIP catalogue record for this book is available from the British Library

ISBN 978-0-7499-4276-2

Typeset in Perpetua by Palimpsest Book Production Limited, Grangemouth, Stirlingshire
Printed and bound in Great Britain by MPG Books, Bodmin, Cornwall

Author's note
I just want readers to know that all the products, books and treatments that I've
mentioned in this book have been paid for by me. There have been no 'freebies'.

Papers used by Piatkus are natural, renewable and recyclable
products sourced from well-managed forests and certified
in accordance with the rules of the Forest Stewardship Council.

Mixed Sources
Product group from well-managed
forests and other controlled sources
www.fsc.org   Cert no. SGS-COC-004081
© 1996 Forest Stewardship Council
FSC

Piatkus
An imprint of
Little, Brown Book Group
100 Victoria Embankment
London EC4Y 0DY

An Hachette UK Company
www.hachette.co.uk

www.piatkus.co.uk

Contents

Acknowledgements

I have so many people to thank that, were I receiving an Oscar, someone would be pulling me off the stage long before I'd finished listing them!

I'd like to start by expressing huge gratitude to my agent Nicola Ibison at First Artist Management – because she was the first person to understand what I was getting at with this book, and she's supported and encouraged me quite brilliantly. She also pointed me in the direction of two wonderful agents at William Morris: Eugenie Furniss and Rowan Lawton. They've been fantastic in their constructive comments and dedication to detail. I could not have got this book off the ground without them. Then – fortunately for me – Eugenie and Rowan found me the marvellous Gill Bailey at Piatkus (Little, Brown) and I am more grateful than I can say that she agreed to publish the book and that she's given me so much enthusiasm and support. I'd also like to thank senior editor, Anne Lawrance for her massive help with the manuscript, and Jan Cutler for her expert copy-editing.

One of the most heartening things about writing *Too Young To Get Old* was the response to the questionnaire that I devised and put on my website. Hundreds of women filled this in and I had some amazing replies. I am particularly grateful to all the respondents who not only took part but subsequently emailed me to say how much they'd enjoyed doing so – and how it had really got them thinking about the future.

On the subject of questionnaires, a big 'thank you' to

Laura Brand for distributing dozens of these on paper in Scotland and the Midlands. Thanks too to my many friends, relatives and colleagues who persuaded contacts of theirs to take part – especially Marcelle Bernstein, Alice Cacouris, Sally Chilton, Tom and Cookie Cotcher, Fiona Dawe, Frances McCabe, Julie Peasgood, Alexandra Webber and Janet Wright. Also, I'd like to thank the female baby boomers among my fellow-players at Badgers Tennis Club in Kemptown, and also the participants in the appropriate age group of the ballet class at the Brighton Marina David Lloyd Club.

I am also particularly grateful to the organisations 50 Connect and Women In Journalism for linking to the survey via their websites. And also to my husband Dr David Delvin for analysing the results, as well as reading and commenting on the manuscript and for bringing me endless pots of tea while I wrote it.

I had help with some of the science from Josh Hulbert and I am indebted to him for his research, as I am to Amanda Kuepfer for her European perspective, and to Lollie Barr for an impression of what goes on 'down under'. Also, to David and Debbie Sharpless for telling me about their Spanish experience.

Now, I'd like to thank the many experts who gave me comments by email, phone or in person – starting with two of my very good friends, Dr Mike Knapton (Associate Medical Director of the British Heart Foundation) and Dr Max Pemberton of the *Daily Telegraph*.

I am also most grateful to Dr Ros Altmann, Jasmine Birtles, Dr Susan Blakeney, Dr Carole Burgoyne, Julia Cole,

Gillian Connor, Dr Carol Cooper, Dr Alan Maryon Davis, Rupert Fisher, Eva Fraser, Simonne Gnessen, Paula Hall, Angela Kilmartin, Denise Knowles, Chris McLaughlin, Dr Rosemary Leonard, Michael Neenan, Thea Newcomb, Professor Jan Pahl, Carl Cutler, Dr Mark Porter, Sian Porter, Marja Putkisto, Dr Gianetta Rands, Yasmin Rumjahn, Leslie Seldon, Dr Alex Shand, Charlotte Stilwell, Malcolm Stuart, Liz Thomas, Professor Alan Walker, Professor Richard Webber, Patsy Westcott and Robyn Vickers-Willis.

I also really want to thank the huge number of vibrant, successful female baby boomers who spared time to help me with comments or observations. They include: Annabelle Apsion, Christine Balian, Tina Baker, Nina Bell, Yasmin Alibhai-Brown, Heather Couper, Janet Ellis, Sarah Little, Carole Malone, Margaret Martin, Jenny Money, Bola Ojo, Felicity Palmer, Sue Paskins, Claire Peligry, Maureen Raynard, Anita Romer and Jane Wheeler.

Too Young to Get Old completely took over my life while I was writing it, and the fact that I had so much encouragement from all quarters was a tremendous bonus. So, to everyone who assisted me in any way at all, can I just say: 'Thanks a million – and let's keep booming and blooming!'

Introduction

Was there ever a luckier generation than ours?

Thanks to Virol, orange juice and the NHS, those of us born between 1945 and 1965 had a healthier start in life than any children before us. We also had free education right through to degree level – courtesy of the 1944 Butler Act – and we even had grants (remember those?) instead of student loans, to fund us through college or university.

The Pill gave us the freedom to be sexy, but not necessarily responsible. Then there was women's lib, which many of us latched on to with alacrity. We may not actually have burned our bras, but we often went without them – delighted with the concept of this freedom even if it was hellishly uncomfortable. We also thrilled to the possibilities that we could make a difference, have a voice, and work in a man's world.

Financially, many of us have been in charge of our own money, which is another first. And years of owning property have allowed us to better ourselves – even if the recession has taken a bite out of what we assumed we had.

Good food became much more plentiful and varied, and exercise more interesting. And just when we thought that things couldn't possibly improve further, someone invented opaque tights. No wonder we're so fabulous!

But now what? Having redefined the rules throughout our lives, it stands to reason that we will want to find a novel way to pass through our vintage years. After all, we're far too young to get old. But what are our options? What do we need to start planning for? And how can we stay in charge of our lives – and, of course, look and feel as young as possible?

These are the questions I've been asking myself – but I've also found that other women are asking me the same questions. As well as being a writer and health journalist I'm a psychotherapist, and I'm finding that more and more baby boomers are coming into therapy to try to sort out where they go from here.

It's one thing embracing the joy of grandchildren and gleefully anticipating free bus travel, but we dread the downsides of the ageing process. In fact, we don't feel ready, because there's still so much we want to do. It's probably true to say that, unlike Miss Jean Brodie, many of us don't even think we've reached our prime yet!

So, we're asking how we're going to carve out a vital, fun and energetic life for ourselves as we approach what previous generations regarded as 'old age'.

Mostly we have no wish to retire – at least not in the conventional sense. True, we may relish the chance to stop our current employment, but we have exciting plans – and we want to be perky and solvent enough to execute and enjoy them. Our mothers might have grown old greyly and gracefully but that is just not us.

For a while now, I've been on the lookout for a book that would give me the lowdown on how to prepare for the next dynamic decades, and which would also enable me to help my boomer clients as they strive to forge the kind of future that appeals to them.

I couldn't find anything suitable, which is why I had to write this book myself!

CHAPTER 1

Let's Keep Rocking and Rolling ...

'You don't get to decide how you're going to die.
Or when. But you can decide how you're going to live now.'
(Joan Baez)

So, the oldest of us are picking up our bus passes and drawing pensions. How on earth did this happen? Many of us don't yet feel old enough to read *Good Housekeeping* or to shop in Jaeger!

It's taken us ages to accept that we're grown up, let alone going to become pensioners. And now that this realisation is beginning to dawn, thousands of us female baby boomers are peering into the future in a slightly bewildered fashion as we ask ourselves how, over about the next three decades, we can continue to have as good a time as possible.

WE JUST FEEL DIFFERENT

The thing is that those of us born in the 20 years or so after the Second World War tend to think of ourselves as a special breed – and certainly very different from anyone who has inhabited this planet before us. Because of that, we don't look to our parents' age group to provide the model for the type of older life we might desire. But then we never really did look to them for guidance – so nothing new there then!

To be fair, we probably all know women in their seventies, eighties, or even nineties whom we admire. Maybe we even hope to turn out like them. I've recently watched a documentary on a dance group called the Company of Elders, where the average age is 79, and I found myself deeply touched and inspired by these people's achievements.

However, although certain individuals might impress us, most of what has tended to happen in old age to previous generations doesn't appeal to us at all. So, en masse, we want to shake the future up and do the next bit of our lives very differently from the way it's been done before.

Already, we know what we *don't* want. No matter how old we get it'll be a definite 'no' to sensible and boring clothes, broad-fitting shoes, hairy chins, and people who call us 'dear', or talk to us in the first person plural. I think that even when we're 90, if anyone dares to suggest: 'we need to have our bath now, don't we?' we'll probably hit them.

As for care homes – they are anathema to us. Many of us have seen our parents languish in such places and our response to their situation is uncompromising: 'I won't be doing that!' we say.

So, we know what we don't want to happen in the next few decades. But as yet we're unsure what the alternatives are. This is true the world over. As Australian psychologist Robyn Vickers-Willis says: 'Mid life is often a time of profound change as we start to look within to determine how we wish to live the second part of our life.'

'The New Old'

This is a report by Demos, the independent think tank and research institute, and was commissioned by Age Concern.

Demos reported that as a generation we will redefine the meaning of retirement. *The New Old* authors (Julia Huber and Paul Skidmore) highlighted the following about us:

'At every stage in their lives, the baby boomers have been at the forefront of radical, social, economic and political change.'

'Baby boomers are the least likely of any age group to agree that it is important to fit in, rather than be different from other people.'

'Only 14 per cent of baby boomers believe that "the people in charge know best" compared with 20 per cent of the younger, and 26 per cent of the older generation.'

'Baby boomers are less likely than younger or older generations to measure success by what they own.'

'Baby boomers have pioneered ethical consumption, with 23 per cent having boycotted a company's produce on ethical grounds compared with only 13 per cent of the older generation.'

'Baby boomers are renowned for two distinctive generational characteristics — individualism and liberalism.'

'Baby boomers are more likely to have signed an environmental petition than any other generation.'

What has made us this way? The truth is that women of our age have had a pretty charmed life compared to our mothers and grandmothers — and we'd very much like that to continue, but it didn't start all that charmingly, did it?

HOW IT ALL STARTED

The beginning for many of us was pretty grim compared with today. True, we had our fair share of fun, and we made our own entertainment and could play, quite safely, out in the street with our friends, but food was awful, houses were cold, and Sundays were boring. That's why Tony Hancock's famous episode about enduring — rather than enjoying — his 'day of rest' was so funny. It was all too dismally true.

In many of our homes, there was a hell of lot of tension too. The war seemed like ancient history to us, but it was very recent and relevant to our parents. And although there had undoubtedly been fear and enormous hardship between 1939 and 1945, many women had enjoyed exciting times which wouldn't have come their way had Hitler never attempted to take over the world. They met people they'd never have encountered in peacetime, and they worked in jobs that wouldn't normally have been available to them.

But, after the hostilities, women mostly reverted to a kind of pre-war scenario of staying at home as ordinary wives and mums. That can't have been easy. And many of them also found it hard to adjust to being with a spouse who had seemed perfect before the war, or during it, but who appeared a rather different guy now he was back in 'civvy street' and dressed in his demob suit.

Looking back to the future

On top of those family tensions, the peace that our dads had fought for was a very fragile and insubstantial thing – and we children were not given the impression that the globe's tenuous grasp on tranquillity was likely to be anything other than temporary. So, our lives often felt bleak and uncertain.

Also, we weren't affirmed in a way that kids are today. We were rarely told we were 'fantastic' or 'wonderful'. Instead, we were subjected to negative comments like 'Don't show me up', or 'Don't get above yourself'. As a result, many of us grew up as rather timid people – and it took a while to overcome that.

THINGS START TO LOOK UP

For those baby boomers whose first memories are of the 1960s, life was getting easier, at least here in the UK. There was much more – and varied – food in the shops. And Prime Minister Harold Macmillan's assertion of 1957 – 'most of our people have never had it so good' – actually began to feel true. Some families even started going abroad for their holidays. But our lives were still far from luxurious, and most people did not have half of what they have today: many families had no car and no record player, and most had no central heating. Microwaves and freezers were still a decade or more away, and the average person didn't feel particularly well off – especially towards the end of the 1960s when the pound had been devalued and the economy was in crisis.

As for those of us whose childhoods were lived out in the 1970s, there was a lot of unrest and strikes, with the three-day week and frequent general elections. Also, petrol prices went through the roof, inflation ran riot, and plenty of dads lost their jobs. So, although a baby boomer can be anyone born between 1945 and 1965 – which means that the oldest and youngest of us have some quite different experiences – it would be true to say that we have loads in common in terms of how we started, how we embraced our opportunities, and, most of all, just how many of us there were.

Do you remember your favourite children's books?

Ballet Shoes
The Chalet School Stories
The Famous Five
Heidi
Just William
The Lion, the Witch and the
   Wardrobe

Little Women
The Railway Children
The Silver Sword
Treasure Island
What Katy Did
The Borrowers

WE JUST KEPT ARRIVING

The term baby boomer was not one we heard at the time. The oldest of us, I recall, were rather unglamorously called 'the bulge' which referred to the burgeoning birth rate.

In 1945, just under 800,000 babies were born in the UK, but in 1947 a massive 1,025,427 of us arrived, followed by a further 985,182 in 1948. The numbers dipped a little during the 1950s, but then built to another peak in 1964, when again over a million children were born.

So, there were an awful lot of us to be kept healthy, housed, fed, clothed and schooled at a time of real austerity. Because of that, most of us remember that although we had treats in our young lives, they were rather sweetly simple. Whereas now a child might be taken to Disneyland Paris or Alton Towers for a birthday celebration, we thought it was pretty special to have chicken for lunch instead of mince!

You're a baby boomer if . . .

. . . you remember the foody treats.

Lots of our treats revolved round food – probably because of our relative poverty and the paucity of choice. In our house, it was a real treat on wintry mornings to have hot milk on our cereal – often Shredded Wheat or Grapenuts. Another treat was to go to the old-fashioned grocer and buy a bag of broken biscuits. Somehow they had much more taste than whole ones.

KEEPING THE FAMILY ENTERTAINED

Entertainment was simple too, and in most homes in the late 1940s and much of the 1950s, the radio – or the 'wireless', as it used to be called – was key to keeping us amused, with programmes such as *The Navy Lark* and *Beyond Our Ken*. We also had our own shows like *Children's Favourites* with Uncle Mac, which played popular songs of the time such as 'The Runaway Train' or 'The Laughing Policeman'.

Of course some of us got addicted to *Woman's Hour* or *The Archers* – and we still are!

Everything changed when a breath of fresh air blew in with Radio Caroline and the other pirate radio ships – and the new DJs like Kenny Everett and Dave Cash. The transformation continued with the Beeb's answer to these commercial upstarts in the shape of Radio One, which was launched in 1967 and which made household names of Tony Blackburn, Alan Freeman and John Peel.

Most exciting of all, was when the family wireless gave way to transistor radios. We were able to have our own personal one, which we could keep glued to our ear, or listen to under the bedclothes.

As for television, for a while it was radio's poor relation. Admittedly, many families got a TV set for the Coronation, but plenty of us didn't have one for ages after that. However, by the time the BBC lost its monopoly and ITV was born, lots more mums and dads were forking out for a 'goggle box'. We could sing along with the adverts. And if we were lucky, we were even allowed to watch *Emergency Ward 10*, which seemed quite racy at the time.

THE TEEN YEARS

Fortunately for us, as we emerged from what were often quite strict, rigid and, frankly, dull junior years into adolescence, we began to sniff the possibility that things were changing for the better. And that's when the 'generation gap' came about. What a well-worn term that became! Coined in the 1960s, it encapsulated the differences between our parents and us. And these differences were huge. Not so much a gap, more a whacking great chasm!

Rightly or wrongly, we felt massively misunderstood by older people, and we were in a hurry: a hurry to become adults, and to do things differently. Certainly, I know I wasn't alone in feeling anxious that somehow the grown-ups would f*** everything up before we got a chance to take over.

As a generation we were collectively terrified at the prospect of a nuclear war that would finish us off before we were old enough to achieve anything. And those of us who can remember the Cuba missile crisis of 1962 know that we very nearly had it.

So, probably, it was our common fears, coupled with a belief that we could do much better than the grown-ups, which bound our age group together in a quite extraordinary way.

Politics and us

Specific events – such as the Russian invasion of Czechoslovakia, the student protests in France in 1968, the Ban the Bomb marches, and the Vietnam War – turned us into much more political animals than our mothers had tended to be. We were agitating and planning to take over – and we had no interest in being pale imitations of the older generation or of accepting the status quo.

Our early childhoods had not seemed like much fun. And although some of us really enjoyed school, we didn't subscribe to the notion that these were the 'best days of our lives'. We had bigger ideas and we could see that being adults would give us loads more control and choice. We had an opinion on everything, and became rebels with masses of causes – the main ones being the pursuit of peace, and shrugging off the old order.

Do you remember these life-altering dates?

1959–79 (approx.): Vietnam War

1961: Pill approved for use in the UK

1962: Beatles record their first single

1967: Abortion Act (came into effect on 27 April 1968)

1968: Thanks to Mary Quant, the mini-skirt became popular nationwide

1969: Divorce Reform Act

1969: First man walks on the moon at 2.56 GMT on 21 July

1969: Representation of the People Act – giving the vote to 18-year-olds (previously you had to be 21 to vote)

1971: Decimalisation in the UK

1972: *Cosmopolitan* magazine, edited by Joyce Hopkirk, appeared on our news-stands in March and changed our lives forever. (It had already taken off in the US where Helen Gurley Brown had transformed an existing magazine with that title into the must-read mag for sassy young women.)

BREAKING AWAY

Meanwhile, in contrast to all that serious stuff, we were beginning to enjoy the adventure of dressing very differently from our mothers, and doing our hair and make-up in ways that our parents found bizarre and bewildering. Indeed, we were the first generation not to look like a cut-down version of Mum. I had friends who were able to do a passable impression of Jean Shrimpton, who, you may remember, was the top model of the early to mid 1960s. She was gorgeous, with her elfin face and loads of eye make-up and nude lips. Alas, for one very uncool teenager, there was no hope of getting my hair to be like hers, and I was not allowed out of the house with anything more than a whisper of mascara. Mine was a tragic life! I wasn't any better at looking like Twiggy either, as I had far too many curves.

We funded our forays into fashion with our Saturday jobs in Freeman, Hardy and Willis, Dolcis or Marks &

Spencer. What joy it was to be able to purchase our own shoes – and ignore the adults who told us that they'd ruin our feet. We could buy mini-skirts too. And long white boots. Or, later, tank tops and flares, and psychedelic prints. And, of course, we had our own music – which was invariably loathed by our parents.

These common experiences and developments, which defined us baby boomers, created a bond among us all, and rendered us much less class-ridden than previous generations. Whether we were the daughter of a deb or a dustman, we were all wearing the same trendy gear and practising new dance moves with our mates before going out to our youth club, or the Palais or Locarno on a Saturday night. We would draw inspiration from *Ready Steady Go!* and *Top of the Pops* as we perfected the Shake or the Locomotion.

We were also going into record shops and hogging the booths while we listened to the latest releases. Or we would be sitting around in coffee shops such as the Kardomah and putting the world to rights.

And we had a new slang. Good things were 'cool' or 'groovy' or 'swinging', and bad things were a distinct 'drag' or 'dodgy'.

BEST OF ALL, THE FOOD CHANGED TOO

When I went to a Wimpy Bar for the first time, it seemed like the height of sophistication! It was all so different from roasts at the weekend, cold cuts on Mondays, shepherd's pie on Tuesdays . . .

To be fair, though, I think our mums started to be a bit more experimental too – although with varying results. My mother was really an academic and career woman trapped in a stay-at-home situation. Later, when I was in my teens, she trained as a teacher and became much happier. But I suspect that before that, she felt deeply frustrated, which was probably one reason why she struggled with home-making and cooking, and was in no way 'a natural' in the kitchen.

She did try though, and occasionally would have a burst of creativity and enthusiasm. Alas, this was usually a disaster – particularly her invention called 'Saturday Surprise'. This was a mixture of corned beef, or tinned salmon, or sausages, with mashed potato on top and various other additional 'surprises' according to her mood on the day. There might be lumps of curry powder in it, or a mash-up of carrots and bananas. And it was quite frequent for her to crush some cornflakes on top of the dish in the mistaken belief that they were much the same as toasted breadcrumbs. Imagine if you will the combination of the weird sweet-ness of cornflakes, plus chunks of oily salmon, lumps of margarine-tasting mashed potatoes, and a morsel of banana . . . downright diabolical!

Of course, I can see now that it must have been ghastly for her to have to produce meals every day for a husband who was notoriously difficult to please, plus three com-plaining kids.

Luckily – courtesy of our increasingly ethnically diverse society – we began to have some exotic choices on the rare occasions that we ate out, as Chinese, Indian and Italian restaurants sprang up in many parts of Britain. And it wasn't only the food that was different. The people running these establishments were clued up to the fact that we might conceivably want to eat out on a Sunday, or late in the evening – and were industrious and flexible enough to stay open at these usually 'dead' times. Hallelujah!

Do you remember your favourite films?

Blow Up	A Hard Day's Night
Butch Cassidy and the	Mary Poppins
Sundance Kid	M*A*S*H
A Clockwork Orange	My Fair Lady
The Exorcist	One Flew Over the Cuckoo's
The Godfather	Nest
Goldfinger	The Sound of Music
The Graduate	The Sting
Grease	2001: A Space Odyssey

EXPANDING CHOICES – FOR SOME

So, life in general was picking up no end. We were responding to all the changes about ourselves and our own growing list of opportunities, and we were becoming bolder and casting off the attitudes of the past and the timidity that had been thrust upon us.

It's important to recall, however, that we didn't all feel that life was opening up for us in a remarkable way. Much still depended upon what your father did for a living, where in the country you lived, and how your education was going.

Only a very fortunate 15 per cent of us had got into grammar schools. Clearly, if you hadn't, and your dad had an unskilled job, then the bold new world didn't feel nearly as accessible as it was becoming to those of us who'd somehow managed to pass the dreaded 11-plus and whose parents were better off.

Frances McCabe, who rose to become a senior civil servant at the Department of Health, remembers: 'Most of the girls I knew on our council estate were not coached by their families to get into grammar schools, and they had to fight hard if they were to have a career rather than some sort of dead-end job just till they got married.' She went on:

> *I became a nurse. But my father wouldn't allow me to leave home to do that. In fact, when I went for an interview to a large teaching hospital some 30 miles from where I lived, they insisted that a parent came with me. And after they'd interviewed me, they spoke to my dad on his own — and when he said he needed me at home, that was the end of that! I had to train in my hometown at a smaller hospital. I suppose I was lucky he let me do nursing at all. Dad didn't believe in careers for women and told me once that my job was 'to breed'. So it took us working-class kids longer to join in that social revolution.*

The strange thing was that many of the posher girls got left behind too. Having interviewed large numbers of women for this book, I've realised that those of us who hailed from the poorer ends of the middle classes often found it easier to grab the new opportunities than those born further up the social scale.

Naturally, some upmarket teenagers did go to university and become lawyers and doctors. However, in many classy homes, the parents' view of a woman's role was identical to that of Frances McCabe's dad. And if they didn't actually say: 'All a woman is good for is for breeding', you can bet your life that that's what they thought.

A colleague who went to an elite fee-paying school says that there was still huge emphasis on the girls in the family making a good marriage.

Knowing how to nurture a man, keep house, cook the perfect soufflé and host dinner parties to bolster your husband's career were still seen as the key skills that would carry you through life, and ensure you were provided for.

But for those of us who did go to university or college – even though for many timid girls from the provinces this was a terrifying thing to contemplate – life did begin to open up in a most exhilarating way, partly, of course, because many educational establishments were new and fresh, and different-looking. In particular, the six 'plate glass' universities (East Anglia, Essex, Kent, Lancaster, Sussex and York) seemed to cast off the fuddy-duddiness of the past and stand as statements to a sprauncier new order.

AND WHAT DID WE BECOME?

One of the questions I've put to masses of female baby boomers is this: 'What would your ten-year-old self make of the person you've become?' And practically everyone I've asked has answered: 'She'd be amazed.' Isn't that great?

And these amazing lives went off in so many different directions that I think for 25 years or so we probably didn't think too much about which generation we came from and what we have in common with each other. We've been far too busy juggling our time, carving out our respective roles and doing our own thing.

The books that changed us

The Book of Love

Fat is a Feminist Issue

Fear of Flying

The Female Eunuch

The Feminine Mystique

My Secret Garden: Women's Sexual Fantasies

Superwoman: Every Woman's Book of Household Management

The Women's Room

Zen and the Art of Motorcycle Maintenance

The Joy of Sex

Happy families

Those of us who are the oldest post-war boomers tended to marry youngish, and had babies quite early – although this by no means applied to us all. Some of us just never got round to having children – or even decided to abstain from parenting because the planet seemed too overcrowded already.

Then those women born after about 1960 often became mums at an older age – but again, although this was the norm, there were plenty of us deviating from it.

Most of us have worked. Many of us have started businesses — and a sizeable number have ventured into careers
that were previously commandeered by men. But some of
us haven't actually chosen to live all that differently from our
mothers — except maybe that we've had more sex, and more
partners, and often stepchildren or step-grandchildren too.

Sharing challenges

So, despite having had a real bond as teenagers, and a
feeling that we were 'all in this together', we were certainly
not a homogeneous group during our late twenties, thirties and early forties. But because we're now all beginning
to face similar challenges, there is a real sense that we're
coalescing again in mid life. And it's a comforting, stimulating and intriguing sensation.

WHAT NOW?

Look around you at the women who have risen to the top
in our generation. What are their attitudes to life now?
Because whatever they are, the rest of us will probably try
to follow. Frankly, I can't see Janet Street Porter becoming
a sweet old lady. I doubt if Susan Sarandon is going to sit
in a rocking chair and knit socks. I'm sure that Lesley
Garrett will never be dowdy. It's inconceivable to think
that Martina Navratilova might ever become fat or twee.
And I'm convinced that Madonna will be a sex symbol
until she falls off the perch.

As for one of our greatest role models — Dame Helen
Mirren — we just know she will never become pathetic. In

a recent interview, she talked about how a man who had not recognised her, offered her his seat on the bus. She accepted graciously and thanked him. But felt absolutely mortified.

She's not alone. Plenty of us fancy a sit down on public transport, but we don't want anyone to think we're frail enough to need it!

Saying it how it is

The truth is that we don't tend to feel we've changed much in the last 30 years, but even the most optimistic of us realises we'll change a bit in the next 30. And it occurs to me that if we want to continue to be viewed as the vibrant, energetic women that we are – and to redefine the next period of our lives – we may need to let other individuals know how we expect to be treated.

Recently, I had a letter from Boots the chemists to come for an eye test. Initially, it just seemed like the normal invitation to check whether or not my reading glasses were still up to the job, but I quickly realised that it was couched in different, gentler terms from usual and seemed a mite patronising. And at the bottom, there was an appointment card stuck to the letter, with the suggestion that I might perhaps like to make a note on that card about when the appointment was to be.

I was puzzled until I realised that having recently had a 'big birthday', Boots now appeared to regard me as 'elderly'. Unbelievable! So I trotted round to my local branch and pointed out that I belong to the 'sex, drugs and rock 'n' roll' generation and had not as yet any inclination to take to my bath chair. Will my admonishment make any difference? Probably not, but it made me feel better!

And I shall continue to fight against being pigeonholed in some category where I don't feel I belong.

Those ghastly labels

I don't know about you, but I've no wish to be referred to as a 'silver surfer', and I wince at the idea of being labelled 'elderly' or a 'pensioner'. I have also vowed not to indulge in 'senior moment' jokes like: 'I couldn't find my spectacles, which led to me tripping over the dog and banging my head, so I went to bed to recover, but, guess what, I lay down on my glasses, which had been in my pocket all the time, and broke them. You had to laugh . . .'

Actually, I think that terminology is one of the things that – given our force of numbers – we will probably change. We're not a generation noted for euphemisms. So when the time comes, I think we may well opt to be called 'old' rather than 'elderly' or 'aged'.

And when people die, I expect us to say just that, and not get into tortuous phrases about them having 'departed' or 'passed over'. We might even find a brand new word for 'retirement'.

THE FUTURE BECKONS

To find out more about where we are currently, and what we want and what we most fear, I devised a questionnaire. It has now been answered by hundreds of women worldwide, and the results of this survey give a fascinating snapshot of the female baby boomer in mid life. It's included below. Do fill it in, if you'd like.

Rather gratifyingly, many women who filled it in emailed me to say that appraising their life in this way had got them thinking about the next decade or so. And I've come to believe that that is precisely what we need to do: we need to start thinking and planning for the future – if it's to be the one we want. And we ought to be getting on with it.

QUESTIONNAIRE

1 Do you live in the UK?

2 How old are you?

3 How old do you feel (in years?)

4 How old do you think you might live to?

5 What is/was your occupation?

6 What's the best thing about growing older?

7 Are you in a live-in relationship?

8 Do you have children?

9 Do you have stepchildren?

10 What are your current ambitions?

11 What do you fear most about getting older?
(You can tick/highlight more than one answer.)
a) Becoming immobile
b) No longer having control of your life

c) Losing your mind
d) Being lonely
e) Running out of money
f) Getting seriously ill
g) Other – please explain

12 Are you happier now than when you were younger?

13 How many real friends do you have?

14 When did you last make a new good friend?

15 Do you see/contact your friends regularly?

16 Do you still have plans to change your life?

17 How regularly do you exercise?
a) 30 minutes a day
b) A few times a week
c) I keep active – have a dog, etc
d) I'm a bit of a couch potato

18 Do you eat with your health in mind – that is, bearing in mind your cholesterol, blood pressure, any tendency to heart disease in your family, and so on?
a) Yes, definitely
b) Mostly
c) Sometimes
d) No

19 Is sex still important to you?
a) Definitely
b) Quite
c) Not much
d) No
e) Might be if I got a new partner!

20 Are you:
   a) Heterosexual
   b) Lesbian
   c) Bisexual

21 Where do you hope you might be living when you die? (You can tick/highlight more than one answer.)
   a) In my own home
   b) In a care home
   c) In warden-assisted housing
   d) With one of my children
   e) In a hotel
   f) Other – please explain

22 Finally, in a sentence or two, please describe how you plan to live your life over the next 30 years or so.

What the survey revealed

The most marvellous and heartening result from the survey is that virtually 70 per cent of us are happier now than when we were in our teens or twenties. Here are some of the other findings that leapt out at me:

- We baby boomers mostly feel young for our age.
- On average, we view ourselves as being 16 years younger than we really are.
- The thing we value most about the age we are now is self-confidence.

- Other things we love are increased wisdom, more freedom – and bus passes!
- Our greatest fear is of becoming immobile.
- We also worry about losing control of our lives.
- Sixty-five per cent of us are anxious about getting dementia.
- Only one-third of us fear loneliness.

Actually, my overall sense when reading through all the questionnaires was that many of us feel we're just beginning to get things right, and that it's taken a while to get to the point where we like ourselves and feel confident. And we're keen for it all to go on for a bit longer, thank you very much!

However, although the survey also showed that we have loads of ambitions, many of these are rather vague and non-specific, and as yet not planned for in any serious way; for example, lots of women wrote that they intended to live with friends at some point in the future. But how easy would that be to arrange? Perhaps it's time to find out.

I think, too, that we need to start asking ourselves which of our ambitions we genuinely wish to achieve, and once we've decided, draw up a goal-list and schedule. As a therapist, I can tell you that regret is one of those emotions that really gnaws away at people: not the kind where you wish you hadn't done something – like getting drunk at your son's wedding – but the sort that arises from leaving things undone that you really wanted to do. Let's not have that regret.

Planning ahead

Now, there are, of course, associations – such as Age Concern – who have lots of information that could help us plan our futures. But the fact is that we're not calling them. And I think that's because we still feel invincible and don't think that any organisation with the words 'age' or 'aged' in the title could possibly have anything to do with us. In fact, a press officer at Age Concern told me: 'Although the services we offer might be suitable for people in their fifties and early sixties, they don't see themselves as "older people" or "pensioners". From our experience we know that our service-users are usually over 65, and their needs are very different from baby boomers'.'

And the situation is similar on the other side of the Atlantic. An American doctor told me that the AARP (American Association of Retired Persons) has struggled to get baby boomers interested in joining it.

I confess that I've always felt I'd sooner pull my fingernails out one by one than ring up Age Concern. Obviously, I'm not alone. I must admit at this point, however, that because of writing this book, I *have* called them. Interestingly, my fingernails are intact! More than that, I discovered that they have masses of advice that might help us. So, what I'm going to do in the next 11 chapters is to look at all the aspects of our lives and to gather together as much useful information as I can – including from organisations with 'age' in the title! – in order to help us rise to our next big challenge, which is to live our future as amazingly as we've lived our past.

CHAPTER 2

Too Young to Retire

'Retirement at 65 is ridiculous. When I was that age,
I still had pimples!' (George Burns)

When you were small, what did you want to be when you grew up? If people asked me that question, I used to say 'a nurse' or 'a mummy' or 'a lady who works in a sweet shop'! Maybe your ambitions were similar — after all, those were the things we knew about.

Fast forward to now, and it's utterly staggering what we've achieved. In my survey I counted well over a hundred different occupations — including architecture, engineering, garden design, politics, professional music-making, publishing and science. There was even a vintage aeroplane restorer!

How times have changed. When we left school, many of us settled for nursing, teaching or secretarial work, because that's what women did. Jan Cutler, who has been the copy-editor of this book, remembers applying to train as an antiques restorer only to be told that as they didn't have a ladies' toilet, they couldn't consider her application.

We've developed in a myriad of different directions through the decades – and many of us have really loved being in the workplace. Fiona Dawe, Chief Executive of Youthnet, says: 'I had no clear idea of what I'd do in life, except I did know, once I started work, that I was *good* at work!'

Much to our delight and surprise, many of us found the same. In fact we like work so much that we're not content with one job. Masses of women who answered my questionnaire are combining at least two careers. So, quite apart from all our other triumphs, we're also responsible for the concept of 'Portfolio Living'.

BUT WHAT HAPPENS NOW?

Unfortunately, the current job situation is far from rosy. So, is luck finally running out for us baby boomers? We've been colossally fortunate so far, but unemployment is rising – and at the same time many of us have seen our pensions, property and savings lose value. As I write this, the economy is improving, but there's little doubt that it'll take ages to get back to the glory days of the mid-noughties.

This means that we're at a crossroads. Mid life has its challenges at the best of times, but the recession has changed some of our plans just when we thought they were sorted. And how we deal with our employment options over the next few years is going to have a huge impact on how we'll be able to live the rest of our lives.

So, in this chapter, I'm going to look at employment

for baby boomers. Alas, we're too old to be firewomen, which is a pity, as those thigh-wader boots that they wear are awfully fetching! But I think you'll be pleasantly surprised at just how much we can still do – especially if you're only in your late forties or early fifties.

Taking it easy

It's just as well, by the way, that few of us wish to retire, stay home, do nothing and live off our savings – because all the money experts say that this is the worst possible time to do that. Fortunately, only 5 per cent of the women I surveyed were interested in conventional retirement. For most of us, the notion of sloping off with a carriage clock under our arm to a lifetime of tending pot plants feels totally alien. So our choices are to:

- Continue to work at what we're doing, if we can.
- Consider new forms of employment – especially if we've lost a job recently.
- Go temping.
- Transfer our skills into other forms of employment in the hope of finding more satisfaction and/or job security.
- Work for ourselves.
- Make occasional money to fund the things we really want to spend our time on.
- Look after grandchildren.
- Study for further qualifications to improve our career prospects.
- Volunteer.
- Do a combination of any of the above.

Positive thinking

Most of all, we need to view the future positively, as there are always opportunities, even in the direst of situations. As top economist Dr Ros Altmann, says: 'We all know that many of us will not be able to stop working – but maybe this is a bonus. People who work, stay sharper.' She also says that female baby boomers have been pioneers throughout their working lives and that they will now 'lead the way to a new type of life in their senior years by working well into their sixties – and possibly as late as their seventies.'

So, yet again, it looks like we are going to spearhead a whole new shift of attitude about work – partly fuelled by necessity, and partly because we're far too young to get old and do nothing.

Time traveller

Award-winning actress Lindsay Duncan has fulfilled a lifetime's ambition by playing the female assistant to David Tennant's Dr Who at the age of 59!

BUT WILL YOU BE FORCED TO RETIRE?

In 2006, a law was passed which aimed to end 'forced retirement'. But what does that mean in practice? Well, you now have the right to ask your employer if you can stay on after your retirement age. But you don't have the right to insist on a 'yes'. And because of the recession, it might be harder for a while to get a 'yes', if the firm is cutting back on staff.

Your right to work

If you do want to stay at work, here's a bit of ammunition. If any company tries to get rid of a woman before the men's retirement age of 65, this could be seen as age discrimination. So we have a reasonable chance of arguing the case for staying on for at least as long as our male counterparts.

And there are likely to be further developments, because a report published by the Commons Work and Pensions Select Committee in July 2009 stated that we should be able to work full- or part-time into our seventies or older – so long as we're fit and able to do so. You can bet your life there will be challenges to this recommendation by various employers, but things are moving in the right direction.

Did you know . . .

. . . that if the retirement age of 65 was enforced in politics, one in eight MPs would have to stand down?

GETTING BACK INTO WORK AFTER LOSING A JOB

It's really horrible to be out of work for any length of time – and very worrying too, as the bills mount up. But if this is your situation, don't despair. Instead, focus on what you're good at. Write a list of your main skills and keep looking at it. And remember that if you're a mum, you're almost certainly a great organiser. Running a household, feeding a family and getting kids to school on time in clean clothes and with their gym kit intact is a major operation.

I know you can feel very low if you keep applying for jobs and don't get them, but try not to take it personally. It's not easy to get work in the current economic climate, and this is true of people of all ages. So keep positive, and try this five-point plan to get you back into the workplace:

1 **Lean on your friends** – that's what they're there for – and also ask them to keep a lookout for work you could do. Sometimes mates might know that someone is leaving their firm and you might be able to get your application in before the vacancy is even advertised.

2 **Keep up to date with the Employment section on the Direct Gov website**. There's advice on it about updating your CV. And you can search for a job in your area in the Jobcentre Plus section. You can also find out about training – such as how to improve your computer skills.

3 **Get online if you're not already**. The Department for Work and Pensions says that eight out of
ten companies now advertise their vacancies on the
Web. If you can't afford a computer, make it a daily
priority to get online at an Internet café or library.

4 **Read the local papers**, which are a good source
of information about vacancies in your area. If you
don't want to buy them, your local library will
have copies.

5 **Register with several local recruitment
agencies** – the more people who know about you
the better. And in particular, get on the books of
agencies – such as Maturity Works or Wrinklies –
who specialise in placing older workers. Thankfully,
more and more employers are realising that by
hiring a baby boomer they'll get someone who
turns up at work on time, is a good organiser, is
disciplined, and is not prone to taking days off
because of rows with the boyfriend.

TEMPING

Even if you're looking for a permanent job, don't rule out
temping. Perhaps you think that this is more of a young
person's game, but in fact, the over fifty-fives comprise 22
per cent of the temporary workforce. And temping can
lead to a full-time position once a company knows you.

It can also be a useful option if you're someone who
wants to leave a long-term occupation, but needs to work
intermittently to make ends meet.

WORKING IN A SHOP

What about working in a shop? Even if you haven't done this since your teenage Saturday job, it could be the answer right now – especially as some companies are very boomer-friendly. For example, the Co-op no longer has a contractual retirement age – all they're interested in is whether or not someone is competent to fill a particular vacancy. In fact, they've redesigned their job application forms so that any potential employee's date of birth isn't visible to recruitment managers.

────────── **BABY-BOOMER FACT** ──────────

If you ever shop in B&Q, you may have noticed that more than 25 per cent of their workforce are over 50. Leon Forster-Hill, the firm's diversity manager, says, 'Older workers have a great rapport with the customers as well as a conscientious attitude and real enthusiasm for the job.'

Many individuals who have left stressful and mentally demanding employment find it pleasant to work in a shop for a change. And there are also good opportunities to work part-time, which might suit you if you're just looking for enough money to cover your costs while you start your own business or launch some other exciting plan.

TEACHING – AND OTHER WORK IN SCHOOLS

One exciting plan you might have is to train as a teacher. Many of us were truly inspired by school mistresses in our youth, especially when they encouraged us to get out there and seize life by the throat at a time when our mums and dads were often more timid in their expectations.

When we've had good experiences with teachers, it's natural to wonder if we too could have that kind of satisfying influence on young people.

Another plus for teaching is that it offers job security – and at times like these that's important. Also, many of us have skills in subjects that would be valued in the teaching profession.

So, could this be an option for you? If you're considering it, here are two great pieces of news:

1 In June 2009, the UK government launched a campaign to train 100,000 more teachers.

2 You can train to be a teacher right up until your late fifties. And although the mandatory retirement age for teachers is 65, there are various ways in which they can continue working beyond that, for example through supply teaching.

So, if you're still only 50, you could be looking at a possible 20 years in the profession.

If you're interested, look at the TDA (Training and Development Agency for Schools) website. It has a Way into

Teaching section, in which you can discover how your experience will be taken into account when assessing how much teacher training you'll need. There's also advice on funding.

Teaching assistants

If you don't want to be a qualified teacher, but would like to be a teaching assistant, the TDA website will tell you about that too. And assistants often work until much later in life; in fact the oldest one on record is 93!

Don't forget that no school can operate without a whole bunch of support staff – such as administrators, librarians, dinner ladies, nursery nurses and technical support staff. You can find out about those kinds of opportunities from the TDA too.

THE NHS

Another way you could combine job satisfaction with job security is by working for the health service.

———————— **BABY-BOOMER FACT** ————————

The NHS is the biggest employer in Europe – and almost 80 per cent of its employees are women.

Now, if you watch *Casualty* or *Holby City* on the television you could be forgiven for thinking that the hospitals only employ doctors, nurses and the odd porter. But there are loads of other occupations within the NHS – about 350 at the last count! And a quick glance at the NHS Careers website revealed lots of interesting options to me –

including becoming an art or occupational therapist, dental hygienist, donor carer, groundswoman or dietetic assistant. Honestly, there were jobs I'd never heard of. Why not take a look at what's on offer?

NHS Career's policy is that there's no upper age limit to commencing training. But they do say, 'If you haven't worked in healthcare before, it is wise to get some work experience or voluntary work in your area of interest to satisfy yourself this is the career you want to follow, and to emphasise your commitment to your training.'

There's another useful website called NHS Jobs where specific vacancies are advertised. Again, you'll be amazed at the variety of positions that are there. And if you spend some time using the Advanced Search facility on the site, you should come away with masses of ideas.

And finally on the subject of health, you can train as a doctor on a graduate-entry programme up to the age of 50. And there's no upper age limit to train to be a nurse, although you would have to pass a fairly stiff medical. But this does mean that if you wanted to be a nurse when you were a little girl, and somehow never managed it, then possibly you still can.

WORKING FOR YOURSELF

Let's now look at self-employment. Many of the women I interviewed in connection with this book told me that they'd really had enough of being an employee and of making money for other people, and planned instead to start working for themselves.

Of course, lots of us are self-employed already, which is yet another difference between ourselves and our mothers, who rarely fell into this category. Getting started is probably the hardest bit, but the joy of working for yourself is that you can begin in as small a way as suits you – perhaps while you're still in full- or part-time employment.

- You may have a skill for cooking, or for making beautiful waistcoats or baby clothes – or for doing up houses.
- Most people get established initially by selling their expertise to friends or local people. Is there a craft shop or craft fair near you, or a farmer's market? Could you take a stall? Or share one with a similarly creative friend?
- Or perhaps you have a dog and could walk other people's pooches as well as your own – and gradually build up a canine grooming and exercising empire.
- Maybe you're brilliant at sewing alterations and could do them for friends or the local dry cleaners. You might do so well that you'll be able to open your own shop.
- Another popular business for boomers is to become a doula: someone who gives support and care to other women while they give birth. Now that so many mothers are having babies miles, or even countries, away from their own mums, this is a burgeoning business. And you can train as one even if you've never given birth yourself.

- Or, what about something entirely different, like becoming a Humanist Celebrant – a minister entitled to conduct weddings, naming ceremonies and funerals for individuals who don't want anything connected with formal religion? Again, you'll be getting in on a growing trend – and you can do it at any age.

- Another really great option is to train to become a counsellor or therapist. Women in mid life are ideal candidates, and you can train at any age. A friend of mine qualified on her sixtieth birthday. Once you're trained, you can practise from home. However, there are many different types of counselling and psychotherapy, so you need to do your homework before you decide on which training scheme to do – or part with your hard-earned cash.

  I'm sorry to say that there are plenty of counselling centres whose main interest is in getting hold of your money rather than furthering your career. So my advice is to contact the BACP (British Association for Counselling and Psychotherapy), as they're very clued up about training and all the different ways in which you can do it with reputable organisations.

Change of name - change of career

The author now known as Nina Bell, transformed her life at 50 by going to a new publisher and – having previously focused on non-fiction and journalism – is now writing novels. She says: 'It's been liberating to adopt a new name and a new style and a new persona.'

Nina expects to write for at least another 20 years. 'After all,' she says, 'just looking round my study, I can see books by Ruth Rendell, P. D. James, Fay Weldon, Jilly Cooper, Penny Vincenzi, Elizabeth Jane Howard and Lynda La Plante – and that's just on one shelf!'

Using your home as a business

So far, we've looked at a number of businesses you could run from home, but what about turning your home into your business? Here are a few people who have done just that:

- Lecturer and divorcée Sue Fielding wanted to keep her largish family house after her marriage ended, so she starting letting out rooms to students.
- Joan McDermott found that because her home was near to a major touring theatre she could run a bed-and-breakfast business for the actors.
- Sally Chilton, who was left with little training and no qualifications when her husband ended the marriage, turned her property into a business by taking in lodgers. Today she and a colleague run a successful bed-and-breakfast agency offering a high

standard of accommodation for business people, tourists and interns.

Your house could also provide you with the ideal premises to become a child minder.

─────────── **BABY-BOOMER FACT** ───────────

It might surprise you to know that 25 per cent of child minders are aged 45–54 and that 10 per cent are over 55.

As long as you can pass a medical and make your house child-friendly, you have a good chance of getting your business going – and you are paid an hourly rate per infant. The National Child Minding Association will give you the information and help you need.

Earning money from your car

Another asset you could use to work for yourself is your car. So, how do you fancy becoming a cabbie? According to a female driver at my local company, any woman with a clean licence, a brain and a suitable vehicle that's less than five years old could do it. What you have to do is to register with the Taxi Licensing Office in your hometown or city and they'll give you all the information you need.

It'll cost you about £80 to take a special driving test, and some £450 to get your Hackney Carriage Driver's Licence. You'll also have to pay for a stringent medical and insure the car, as well as adding a meter to it. But, if you like driving, you might really enjoy it. You'll be attached to a local company, but will be self-employed and it'll be up to you what hours you work.

Have you ever considered becoming a bus driver?

Many companies will train you up to the age of 64!

Finding out more

Those are just some of the possibilities you might explore if you want to work for yourself. And whatever type of business you decide to go for, there's plenty of help around for women who want to start up on their own. A good place to get advice, support and information is the Direct Gov website. Another great organisation is PRIME, which stands for the Prince's (that's Prince Charles) Initiative for Mature Enterprise. On that website, you'll find a heading called Case Studies and you can inspire yourself with stories of people of 50 and over who have started their own businesses – and a new way of life.

THAT LITTLE EXTRA

And how about earning a little bit of 'extra' cash?

Whether you're out of work, starting up a business, or just considering your options, it's always good to know about additional ways in which you can earn extra cash from time to time.

Make extra from being an extra

Have you ever pictured yourself propping up the bar in *Eastenders*? Or sitting in swanky clothes in a casino shot in a Bond film? Or being part of a terrified throng in a *Doctor Who* episode? Then try registering with an agency who provide background actors for TV and film.

The upside is you'll meet some stars. The downside is that the hours can be long and tedious – but you might make a £100 in a day.

A good way to start is to buy a book called *Contacts*, which has listings of reputable agencies. You can get it from Amazon, or through Spotlight, the casting directory organisation.

Think outside the box

What about becoming a mystery shopper? These are people who go into stores incognito and report back on how they were treated as customers. It's only occasional work, but there are definitely worse ways to make a few bob.

Or you could offer your housekeeping talents to a busier friend who might be only too pleased to pay you to do her washing and ironing, or to stock her freezer with delicious home-cooked casseroles.

We nearly all have skills that other people would like to purchase. So have a think about what yours are – and earn some dosh.

GRANDPARENT CARERS

Caring for grandchildren can be another way to make some money – but all too often, baby boomers end up giving away their services for a paltry sum, or even for free.

Having grandchildren is one of the real bonuses of getting older: masses of women who took part in my survey told me just how much it meant to them to be a granny. However, it's one thing to enjoy your young relatives every now and then, and quite another to look after them daily. Increasingly, however, that's what our sons and daughters are asking of us. In fact, since the beginning of the economic downturn, 44 per cent of parents have turned to grandparents for help with their offspring.

So, what can you do if you're being asked to do this – and you're not sure that you want to? There is no easy answer, I'm afraid, but try asking yourself the following questions before you decide:

1 Do you have the physical and mental energy to look after these kids every day?
2 Can you afford to do it – especially if your children can't pay you?
3 Are you going to feel resentful if you agree to do it because you really want to get on with your own plans at this point in your life?
4 Is there another way of solving the childcare problem – perhaps with you contributing to nursery fees, or getting other family members involved so that you aren't the only carer?

One glimmer of help is that in the 2009 Budget, Chancellor Alistair Darling announced that women looking after a grandchild of under 12 for at least 20 hours a week would be entitled to National Insurance credits. In other words, you'll no longer lose out on building up your state pension entitlement if you're looking after your grandchildren, as opposed to going out to work.

Even so, this is a tough decision – so don't rush it. The organisation Grandparents Plus is lobbying for more rights for grannies, and you can contact them for help.

STUDYING

Our generation has been excellent at grabbing educational opportunities, but is there still time to get qualifications that might improve your job prospects or launch you on an entirely new career? The answer to that is a resounding 'yes!' – particularly if you're a younger boomer:

- You could begin by finding out what courses your local job centre or council are offering. Often there are classes to help you update your computer skills. Though we often have a love/hate relationship with new technology, there's no doubt that if we want employment – or we wish to work for ourselves – the more computer literate we are the better.
- Learn Direct, which offers online distance learning, is another good place to start. In 2009, some 35,000 over fifty-fives registered with them.
- Then there's the Open University, which has transformed the learning landscape in this country.

~ Case Studies: Tanya and Alyson ~

Forty-six-year-old Tanya Williams from Kent was in banking when she started to study with the OU. Now, she's working at a local college as a programme co-ordinator and has recently completed a master's in Education. She says:

Not bad for a girl who left school with some really poor exam results.

Alyson Smith, 49, from East Sussex used to work for her local council, but after studying with the OU, she's now a teaching assistant in a primary school, and her next plan is to do full teacher training.

If the OU isn't your thing, you could consider actually going to university. Nowadays, women well into mid life are taking diplomas, and undergraduate and postgraduate degrees. Every university has a website, and you can browse through it, looking at possible subjects and finding out how to apply.

So, no matter what you want to do – and at what level – there's something for you. I want to finish this particular section with one of the many inspirational stories I've come across while writing this book.

∼ Case Study: Anita ∼

Anita Romer already had a degree in botany and bacteriology and a PhD in virology before she had children. She told me:

> *Then, when my kids were small, I started a playgroup in my home, to which my own children came. When the youngest was four we both went to a teacher-training college in Newcastle, him to the crèche, me to re-train. I was a secondary school teacher for 17 years. Later, I joined an art club and took an A level in fine art.*
>
> *I'd caught the academic bug again! So, I enrolled on a degree course at Newcastle/Sunderland University part-time. Six years later, in 2005, I gained an honours degree in fine art. The following year, I did a ceramics course and made tiles and plates. The next year I did an illustration course and produced 40 plus watercolours of medicinal herbs.*

Two years ago, I put my name forward to be a local borough councillor for the Lib. Dems and was elected.

There are some amazing women out there!

Carry on achieving

These people have not let age get in their way:

- Hillary Clinton became the US Secretary of State at 61.
- Dame Helen Mirren picked up an Oscar for Best Actress for her performance in *The Queen* when she was 60.
- Felicity Palmer, now in her mid-sixties, is one of Britain's top classical singers, and is still regularly appearing in prestigious opera houses such as The Met and Covent Garden.

  She says: 'I've been enjoying the past 10–15 years more than I did the earlier part . . . I know better what I am doing, perhaps.'
- Lynn Truss – after years of being a great jobbing journo, but not especially famous – wrote best-seller *Eats, Shoots and Leaves* in her late forties.
- Jane Winkworth, founder of the French Sole shoe company, who's in her mid-sixties, is still designing her adorable ballet-type pumps – often while sitting up in bed watching *Coronation Street*!

THE VOLUNTARY OPTION

If full- or part-time education doesn't appeal, but you still want to improve your job prospects, one way of doing it is through volunteering. This is because:

1 Employers like to see volunteer projects on CVs, as it tells them a lot about you.
2 Volunteering gives you new skills and can bring structure to your life.
3 You'll feel good about helping others – and this in turn will help you feel more confident and optimistic.

So, how can you get started?

- In the UK, you can get information from Volunteering England, Volunteer Scotland, Volunteering Wales or, in Northern Ireland, Volunteering-NI.
- You can also get great ideas from The Community Channel, which is available both on the Internet and satellite TV.
- Fifty Forward is another wonderful resource. It's part of the Learn Direct organisation and is especially useful if you'd like to be a mentor. Its website has loads of information on how you can do this, and lists different groups of people you can work with, including young mums, homeless individuals, refugees and ex-offenders.
- Another good website is Do It! If you go to the Quick Search button on the home page, they'll offer you 32 different categories of volunteering.

- Then there's CSV (Community Service Volunteers) where you can find out about a vast range of volunteering activities, or even sign up to train in volunteer management.
- More specifically, if you're a professional person and you want to wind down from your present career – or you can't get the job you want at present – an organisation called Reach would like to hear from you. What they do is to match people who have professional skills to voluntary associations that need them.
- Or perhaps you'd like to be a magistrate? To be quite honest, we may not be what a lot of courts are looking for right now – as they're trying to get a diverse mixture of individuals to sit on the bench, including much younger people. However, as such people are often too busy working and bringing up children to volunteer, you might very well be accepted. There's information about becoming a magistrate on Direct Gov and also on the Magistrates' Association website. You can also ring up your local magistrate's court and find out if they're interested in you and what you can offer.
- On the other hand, you may feel that your working life has given you experiences that you could use at board level for a charity. I've discovered that there is as much competition for this kind of voluntary post in some of the most sought-after organisations as there is for paid work! In the past, many boards were utterly male-dominated, so there's a push these days to include far more women.

- If you're interested in health, try approaching your NHS Trust.
- If you're a keen supporter of the arts, you could offer your services to a theatre trust, or opera or ballet company, or some other artistic venture.

Using your business skills

If you're a business person, you're likely to be particularly sought after, but whatever your background, if you want to do voluntary work at board level rather than in a local charity shop or whatever, there are always openings.

One way of finding out what's available is to read the public appointments pages in the broadsheet newspapers. There's also a useful website called Get On Board.

Or you could just contact an organisation you admire and ask how you can help. You may find yourself doing something rather more basic to start with – but they will get to know and appreciate you, and, hopefully, this will be a way to progress to the level you really want.

Volunteering somewhere new

Finally, could this be a good time in your life to do some volunteering abroad? If so, contact either of these two excellent organisations:

1: Gap Year For Grown Ups

If you've ever envied your offspring, as they've told tales of their gap years, this organisation could be just the ticket. It offers a way of travelling while you help other people. You don't in fact have to commit to a whole year; you could actually start by just going for a fortnight. Signing up for a short programme probably wouldn't feel as daunting as a long project might.

I suggest that you read the diaries of women who've been on one of these trips. They're inspiring stuff. Just go to the home page of Gap Year For Grown Ups, and scroll down until you find the heading Career Break Travel Stories.

2: Voluntary Service Overseas (VSO)

It's amazing how many women of our generation take career breaks to go overseas with VSO – or give up work to do it.

~ Case Study: Bola ~

Teacher Bola Ojo took early retirement and then went with VSO to Rwanda for 12 weeks. She said:

I hadn't volunteered before, so I didn't want to launch straight into a long-term role. Twelve weeks would be a taster, giving me the opportunity to do a self-contained piece of work – something that I could confidently start and finish.

Having done her initial 12 weeks, Bola continues to work with VSO and says of volunteering: 'I'd recommend it 100 per cent! It widens horizons, broadens skills, gives you an appreciation of what you've got – and what can be done if you put your mind to it.'

PORTFOLIO LIVING

Lastly, let's look at Portfolio Living. It's so very us, isn't it? Which is probably why many female boomers have embraced this way of working.

Portfolio successes

- Tina Baker, who's a columnist and TV pundit, has trained as a fitness coach specialising in the over 45s. Now, she combines all three careers.

- Pam Rhodes, novelist and long-term presenter of BBC's *Songs of Praise*, now runs a cattery in addition to her other activities.

- Julie Peasgood had a major success in her fifties when she took a break from acting and wrote a successful book called *The Greatest Sex Tips in the World*.

- Agony aunt Virginia Ironside is not only continuing to advise the anguished but she's also presenting a one-woman show called *The Virginia Monologues*.

- Jane Wheeler, who sells her divine knitwear to exclusive shops worldwide, and who is now also a ceramicist – with several exhibitions in prospect – is renovating a house in Spain, which she plans to rent out.

- Actress Annabelle Apsion, best known for playing Monica Gallagher in *Shameless*, is qualified in Rosen Therapy and helps to run the UK Rosen training school.

- Ruby Wax – who had studied psychology at Berkeley decades ago but never finished the course – recently

---

took a diploma in psychotherapy at Regent's College in London and followed it up by studying for an MA in Neuroscience at University College London. She's now blending her psychological skills with her TV-presenting experience in 'Ruby's Room': a series of filmed discussions on mental-health issues on the BBC's well-being website.

• And I added another component to my existing portfolio – of agony-aunting, writing books and doing a bit of broadcasting – by training in psychotherapy.

Other women I know are doing student-type jobs – like waitressing part-time – so that they can follow their dream of taking a degree, writing poetry or starting a business in interior design. And, of course, there are plenty of baby boomers who are combining caring for grandchildren, working part-time, studying at weekends and also making some cash by renting out a couple of rooms in their house.

Lots of us get hung up on what to choose to do in life, but sometimes – with a bit of planning – you really can do it all.

WHERE TO FIND OUT MORE

BACP (British Association for Counselling and Psychotherapy): www.bacp.co.uk; tel. 01455 883300
B&Q jobs: www.jobs.diy.com/jobs
CSV (Community Service Volunteers): www.csv.org.uk
Direct Gov: www.direct.gov.uk
Do It!: www.do-it.org.uk/wanttovolunteer

Doula: www.doula.org.uk

Fifty Forward: www.learndirect.co.uk/fiftyforward

Gap Year For Grown Ups: www.gapyearforgrownups.co.uk;
   tel. 01892 701881

Get On Board: www.getonboard.org.uk; tel. 0800 652 4886

Grandparents Plus: www.grandparentsplus.org.uk;
   tel. 020 8981 8001

Humanism sites: www.humanism.org.uk; www.humanism-
   scotland.org.uk; www.iheu.org

Learn Direct: www.learndirect.co.uk

Magistrates' Association: www.magistrates-association-
   temp.org.uk

Maturity Works: www.maturityworks.co.uk

Mystery Shopper: www.mystery-shoppers.co.uk;
   tel. 01409 255025

National Child Minding Association: www.ncma.org.uk;
   tel. 0800 169 4486

NHS Careers: www.nhscareers.nhs.uk; tel. 0845 60 60 655

NHS Jobs: www.jobs.nhs.uk

Open University: www.open.ac.uk; tel. 0845 300 6090

Prime: www.primeinitiative.co.uk; tel. 0800 783 1904

Reach: www.reach-online.org.uk; tel. 020 7582 6543

Ruby's Room: www.bbc.co.uk/headroom/rubys/

Spotlight: www.spotlight.com

TDA (Training and Development Agency for Schools):
   http://www.tda.gov.uk

Volunteering England: www.volunteering.org.uk

Volunteering-NI: www.volunteering-ni.org

Volunteer Scotland: www.volunteerscotland.org.uk

Volunteering Wales: www.volunteering-wales.net

VSO (Voluntary Services Overseas): www.vso.org.uk

Wrinklies: www.wrinklies.org

WE CAN STILL LOOK FORWARD

As I said at the beginning of the chapter, this period of our working life may well feel tougher than we were anticipating. But we baby boomers are resilient and resourceful women. And no matter how difficult things may seem, it's worth remembering that we still have loads of options open to us, which our mothers could only dream of. We've never been fainthearted – and we certainly won't be now!

CHAPTER 3

Money, Money, Money

'If you want to know what God thinks of money, just look at the people He gave it to.' (Dorothy Parker)

Are you worried about money? Well, join the club! The worldwide recession has made most of us nervous about our financial futures. And our anxieties are fuelled by a constant stream of news headlines saying that the nation will be in hock for a hundred years, and that all our pensions are disappearing down some mystifying black hole. In my own survey, 40 per cent of baby boomers said they were seriously concerned that they wouldn't have enough money to live on as they got older. So, in this chapter I'm going to look at our finances, with the aim of making us all more savvy and solvent.

BROUGHT UP TO BE FRUGAL

One thing that may help us in these difficult times is that many of us were brought up when money was tight. And we also heard stories within our families about the very real poverty that existed before we were born. As a result, we know that no matter how desperate things seem today, we actually live very luxuriously compared with our relatives of two or three generations back.

My Scottish granny was a young mum in Glasgow during the Depression, and my granddad – in common with most of the other men who were employed by the local ship-building industry – was laid off work for years. Life was a terrible struggle and I remember Granny telling me that she used to cry because she couldn't afford to buy her children apples for their tea.

Every time I remember that, it brings tears to my own eyes. For me, it symbolises just how different our lives as baby boomers have been compared with those of women before us.

I also remember, as probably you do, how as children we were taught to be thrifty, and how we put our sixpences and shillings – or if we were very lucky, half crowns – in our money boxes. We had to save hard for anything we really, really wanted, because that was the only hope of getting it.

If you're one of the older baby boomers, you may recall, too, what it was like as young adults to have to manage money before the era of credit cards and ATMs, when you could only get hold of your cash by drawing it out of your own branch of the bank. That wasn't always easy, as these banks were only open between nine and three o'clock on weekdays and for three hours on Saturday mornings. We had to be organised with our dosh. And the discipline we learned then could come in jolly handy now.

WHAT WE'RE GOOD AT

Through the years, many of us have worked and earned quite reasonable money – and far more than our mothers ever did. Also, lots of us have moved house more frequently than women did in the past – and we've often done well out of buying and selling our own homes. This has given many female baby boomers the desire to go into the buy-to-let business – and large numbers of us have achieved it.

We like houses – and we have a talent for renting them out and titivating them, which we really enjoy. Despite a drop in prices during the recession, I think that most of us in this business are in it for the long term. There's no mandatory retirement age for landlords, and this is a form of investment that we understand and are good at.

WHAT WE'RE BAD AT – AND WHY

Apart from property, we're really not great at planning for our financial futures. Maybe it's because, not so long ago, any family assets automatically went to male descendants, so there was little reason for women in the past to 'worry their pretty little heads' about finance.

Also, our dads often took the view that daughters were hopeless at maths, and we believed them, which left us feeling distinctly inferior.

Another thing is that there are plenty of women – even among our achieving generation – who have never had enough spare money to save any significant amount. After all, most baby boomers have taken time out to have babies and to bring them up – so we've just never earned as much as men.

It also seems that we just don't seem to quite have that 'investment gene' that many blokes have. True, we understand property, but most of us wouldn't know a gilt or a bond if it leapt up and bit us on the bottom. As for shares, the vast majority of us don't meddle with them, whereas men often do. Of course that means we don't suffer the same losses when shares plummet, but over the past 35 years, they have outperformed all other forms of investment – including property. And though they took a severe knock in the economic downturn, most experts reckon that long term they'll continue to be the best investment.

When it comes to pensions, far fewer of us have company ones than men do. And those of us who have personal pensions are cautious with them. So when we're asked by our advisers whether we want our pension invested in low-, medium- or high-risk strategies, mostly we feel enormously brave if we mix in a few 'mediums' with the 'lows', whereas men will risk more.

Perhaps most importantly of all, money still seems to belong in a world dominated by men in pinstriped suits

Personal investing

Once the preserve of the professionals, investing in the stock market is now easily available for anyone. But what to invest in, how to invest and how much to invest are the usual questions that spring to mind. For the beginner, the whole scenario can be quite daunting, but there is a vast amount of information available out there. Perhaps the best place to start looking is on the Stock Exchange website which has a huge amount of information, including some for beginners. You might also think about joining an Investment Club, which, basically, is a group of people who pool their money and invest collectively. As we're always reminded: 'the value of your investment can go down as well as up and past performance is not necessarily a guide for the future.' So, get good advice, think about what you want to achieve and don't rush into anything.

and red braces – and its language is not only infuriating but incomprehensible too. I've just had an annual statement from Norwich Union (AVIVA), and the second paragraph reads: 'We are pleased to advise you that the migration of our back-office administration and IT support to Scottish Friendly was delivered successfully and the new platform is available.'

WHAT!!!? What the hell does this mean? Does it matter? Do I need to know? Oh God!

The way we look at money

There's a bit of a 'girl' thing going on here, isn't there? Not only do we feel that the financial world is too male for us, but — as financial adviser Simonne Gnessen says — we view money very differently from the way men do. She says that our relationship with it is much more emotional than theirs, which is one reason why a massive 79 per cent of us shop to cheer ourselves up!

I can certainly remember that when I was in my thirties and very miserable, my spending spiralled way out of control and I ended up in terrible debt. It took ages to get out of it, but at least I did learn — the hard way — that using money as a comfort-fix is total madness.

So, one thing we need to do is to resist that little voice in our head that's telling us 'I deserve that dress' or 'Those shoes will cheer me up'. Instead, we need to comfort ourselves in ways that won't sabotage our bank balance. If we can put a stop to impulsive spending, we can tackle other problems that get in the way of us making the most of our money.

WHAT STOPS US TAKING CONTROL OF OUR MONEY?

Sadly, one of those problems that get in the way of us taking control is our own children. We baby-boomer mums have raised a generation of Kippers: Kids in Parents' Pockets Eroding Retirement Savings! And it's hard to invest for your future if you're funding your adult child in his or her foray into the media, or some other occupation that depends upon parents' sponsorship.

─────────── **BABY-BOOMER FACT** ───────────

Recent figures from the Office for National Statistics tell us that one-third of men aged 25–34, and one-fifth of similarly aged young women, are living with their parents. And who is subbing them? Yes, it's the baby-boomer mum!

So, helping our kids is a mother's natural tendency. But Jan Pahl, Kent University's Emeritus Professor of Social Policy, says: 'This tendency often inhibits saving for a pension, because when a woman has to weigh up whether to put money away for the future, or pay for something her offspring need now, then the pressure of the present usually wins.'

Do you remember . . .

. . . looking after things and being thrifty?

'Make do and mend' was one of our childhood mottos. We learned how to darn socks – although I don't remember using this skill except to get a badge at Brownies! We watched our mums use leftovers in pies, soups and stews – and buy cheap cuts of meat, which could be slowly cooked until they were tender.

We were also encouraged to save our pocket money by means of children's savings stamps with Prince Charles on the 2s 6d ones and Princess Anne on the 6d. So, if we have to economise now, it really shouldn't be too hard for us. We were born to be frugal.

On top of all of that, many of our generation are not only having to fund their children but are also subsidising ageing parents. No wonder we baby boomers are sometimes called 'baby gloomers'!

Getting to grips with it

But lots of us are finding it a real struggle to manage our money. And this struggle is compounded by the fact that, because we often feel inadequate on the subject, we're frightened to even look at the state of our finances. So, we continually put it off.

Now, I bet you know from other aspects of your life that when you put things off, they don't go away.

In my own clinical practice, I have seen just how distressed individuals become when they refuse to square up to a problem – whether it's about money, overeating, drinking too much, or getting out of a redundant relationship. The truth is that while we avoid things, or distract ourselves from them, we don't have peace of mind. In fact, we grow increasingly anxious. So, we need to try to encourage ourselves to face up to the things we have avoided – and that definitely applies to finance.

Many of us are in one of the situations listed below:

- 'I don't know how much money I've got, and haven't a clue whether it's going to be enough for the next 30 years or so.'
- 'I know I'm in debt – but not sure how bad it is.'
- 'I'm someone who's always left finances to my partner.'

- 'I believe I'm powerless to do anything even if my finances are in a parlous state.'
- 'I'm hopeless with money and nothing can change that.'
- 'I used to think that I had a good pension and that my house was worth quite a bit, but I've lost confidence now and just hope that the politicians and bankers will make everything OK again.'

It is a very female thing to fear finance and to avoid looking at your own circumstances in detail. But is this helping you to feel calm? Or is it helping you when you try to plan an exciting future for yourself? No, it isn't.

Do you remember being deemed 'unreliable'?

When I got my first job in television in the late 1970s, I bought my then husband a motorbike on hire purchase. I sent in my application forms to the finance company but they rang me up asking for my husband's details so that he could stand as my guarantor. I pointed out that I was the one paying for the vehicle and that I was the only one of us with a reliable income because he was an actor and currently out of work. That cut no ice with them. He was the man. He was the husband. And he was deemed to be the more reliable!

HOW TO START TO TAKE CONTROL

So, what can you do to galvanise yourself into action? Here's a four-point plan to help you prepare your mind to face up to your finances:

1 Accept that all the time you spend moaning and putting things off, is in fact using up more energy than actually tackling the problem.

2 Give yourself a realistic timetable for getting sorted – breaking it up into manageable steps and building in rewards (that don't involve spending money) every step of the way.

3 If you have thoughts holding you back such as: 'I shouldn't have to do this kind of thing' or 'It's unfair', try asking yourself why you are so different from other people, and whether there's any evidence that you alone in the universe shouldn't have to face up to horrid tasks.

4 Cast your mind back to a previous occasion when you triumphed over what seemed like an insurmountable difficulty. How did you do it? Which of your strengths did you use? What did you tell yourself? The answers to these questions may help you now.

Getting your mindset right is more than half the battle. It will help you to do what money-management guru Jasmine Birtles calls 'facing the tiger'. This means, taking a long, cold look at your finances – perhaps for the first time – and doing a complete assessment of them.

She and all the other financial experts I've spoken to say that there is no real way forward until we've got a clear idea of how things are right now. So, draw up a list of:

1 What you earn.
2 What you owe.
3 What savings you have.

Partners in finance

When you've made your list, if you have a partner, you can go on to look at whether any of his (or her) money is going to be helpful to you.

It's amazing how many of us are unsure whether our partners have made any provision for us – and indeed whether or not a spouse's pension will benefit us, albeit at a lower rate, if he or she dies first. So find out, and add this figure to your assessment.

Inheritance, pensions and property

Next, write down any money that you are sure to inherit. But in the present economic circumstances I suggest you make a very conservative estimate of what that's likely to be.

Also, you need to look at your pension arrangements. Have you got a company pension? A personal pension? Do you qualify for the full state pension?

What about property? Do you own your place? Might you downsize at some point? And do you have other properties? Will you sell them or keep them to make you an income?

Equity release

If you own your house and are approaching retirement, the words 'equity release' may have leapt out at you from various newspapers or television commercials. This is a way of unlocking some of the value of your home. A company will give you ready money in exchange for a share of your property when you die.

This might seem like a very good idea, but is it? You can find good explanations of equity release on websites such as Unbiased, 50 Connect and Saga. But all the experts I've spoken to say that you shouldn't sign up for anything until you've consulted an independent financial adviser who specialises in equity release schemes. Expert Simonne Gnessen says that before you agree to anything, you should ask any adviser you consult to put you in touch with

---

another client who has already gone in for an equity release scheme like the one you're considering. If the adviser is reluctant to do this, go to one who will. Equity release is a big step; it could be just what you need to put your finances back in order, but you want to be sure you're not making a costly mistake.

Calculate your earning and spending years

It would also be useful to work out how many more 'earning' years you think you have – and how much money you might therefore still be able to make.

Another thing to establish is what you spend every month – then you can begin to see how much money you're going to need to live on over the next 30 years or so, and whether or not you're going to have to economise, or to re-think some of your future plans.

Now, making this extensive summary of your financial position could easily take a fortnight to complete. But stick at it. Once you're done, you'll feel a huge sense of relief – even if you don't like what you find. People always deal better with what they know for sure, rather than with what they imagine.

It's possible of course that you'll find that you're better off than you thought. But if you find that things are worse than you feared – well at least from today you can proceed from a position of real knowledge and take steps to get solvent.

GET OUT OF DEBT

When women of our generation face up to the fact that they are badly in debt, they often feel very ashamed – and they keep it a secret. But debt can happen to anyone. Maybe you've got divorced and have ended up much poorer than you once were. Perhaps your partner has been a spend-thrift, and you've been left to pick up the pieces. A friend of mine discovered that her husband of 25 years had a gambling habit, and that their home would have to be sold to pay off his debts. She's now living in rented accommo-dation and struggling to find enough work to get back on her feet. A patient of mine has had several bouts of debil-itating mental illness – and so has found it difficult to hold down a job. And plenty of women have been made redun-dant during the recession and are finding it hard to make ends meet. So, just because you're in debt, it doesn't mean that you're a bad person. Do remember that.

It may be that once you've completed your financial assessment, you'll be able to get yourself out of debt by cutting your spending every month so that it never exceeds your income, and by clearing everything you owe on your credit cards.

Credit-card blues

Many of us think that credit-cards balances don't really count as 'debt', but they do. And they're costing a fortune in interest – especially if you spend to your limit, but only make minimum repayments. If you don't believe me, look through your credit-card statements of the past two years, and add up all the interest you've paid. That's usually a horrendous eye-opener.

The best advice I was ever given was to restrict myself to spending cash while I paid off my credit cards – and from then on to never spend more on cards than I could completely pay off per month.

It took me ages to get to that point. But once I did, it was a massive weight off my mind. So maybe by being really strict with yourself you'll become solvent, but if the problem is too big for you to cope with alone, then go and get help. This doesn't need to be costly. In the UK, you can make an appointment with a Citizens' Advice Bureau (CAB). Or ring their helpline. They are the experts in getting people to be honest with what they owe, what they spend, and what they earn. The CAB also has useful information on their website. Alternatively, you can contact the free and independent National Debtline service.

Don't be a sitting duck!

Whatever you do, don't respond to one of those ads in the papers or on TV that try to persuade you to consolidate all your debts into one big loan. These schemes are all about making money for debt management companies, not for you. Don't touch them!

GREAT WAYS TO CUT DOWN YOUR SPENDING

Whether or not you need expert help to sort out your debt, there are always ways you can cut down on what you spend, and some of them aren't even very painful. Do remember that in the current economic climate, it's fashionable to be thrifty! So, the first thing is to be open with your friends and family and tell them that you're in debt, or just worried about money, and that you're now on a big economy drive. They will admire you for it – and probably join you!

If you look at your own bank and credit-card statements, you'll probably see for yourself how you can cut back. But if you want some more ideas, try these:

1. Give up your car! Work out what it costs you to run per year. Isn't it a lot? Now look into what buses and trains, and even the occasional taxi, would cost you. There'll be a big saving. I reckon that most of us who don't live in rural areas – where cars plainly are a necessity – would be better off if we gave up our 'wheels'. You could also consider joining a car-sharing scheme.
2. Stop automatically paying the bill when you go out with your adult children.
3. Take your own (nutritious) lunch to work.
4. Only have a latte on your commute once a week.
5. Hold a good-as-new clothes sale with your friends. Those shoes you bought that were always too tight could be snapped up by a mate!

6 Get your insurance via an over-fifties organisation. I know we feel far too young to use them, but there are big discounts to be made by admitting your age! Try Saga and RIAS for starters.

7 Carry your own water bottle around rather than buying mineral water.

8 Have a big clear-out at home and either sell all the stuff you don't need at a car boot sale, or have a garage sale. Serve tea and cakes, get lots of friends to help – and watch as the profits roll in.

9 Get freebie doses of culture – music in parks, museums and galleries, and street theatre.

10 Stop eating out with friends. Instead, go to each other's homes and each contribute to the meal.

11 Buy all your day-to-day glasses/crockery/table mats from charity shops. People donate the most fantastic stuff.

12 Buy jewellery and other accessories from charity shops too – you might get some real bargains, especially in upmarket areas.

13 Visit the Love Food Hate Waste website for lots of ideas about buying and eating wisely, using left-overs, and generally saving money.

14 Visit two websites called Love Money and Motley Fool for loads of good economising tips.

15 Whenever you can, shop using cash, and always ask for a discount – because often you'll get one.

16 Look out for deals on utilities. We're not nearly as good as men or younger people at switching suppliers, but this is a great way to save money.

EXPERT HELP

So, far – apart from mentioning the CAB and the National Debtline – I've focused on how you can help yourself. But there is loads of expert advice that you could access to help you – and some of it is free; for example, do you read the business and money sections of your daily newspaper? If you do, give yourself a pat on the back, because you're in a tiny minority. Mostly, we female boomers throw them out – which is a terrible waste. With effort, we can educate ourselves by reading this information.

I would also strongly recommend that you read everything you can that is written by the following people:

- **Dr Ros Altmann**, economist, investment banker and adviser to the pensions industry. Take a look at her website, where you'll find masses of useful information.
- **Jasmine Birtles**, financial journalist and broadcaster. Her website, Money Magpie, covers everything you need to know about finance in a lively and fun way. Also read her informative and easy-to-read book called *The Money Magpie: I Can Help You Ditch Your Debts, Make Money and Save £1000s*.
- **Simonne Gnessen,** independent financial adviser and author. She works in Brighton, but also deals with clients (mostly female) online. Simonne's book, *Sheconomics*, is a must-read – co-authored with Karen Pine who is Professor of Developmental Psychology at the University of Hertfordshire. Simonne's advice also features on the Sheconomics and Wise Monkey websites.

- **Ruth Sunderland**, business editor of the *Observer*. Read her excellent and accessible advice in that paper and on the *Guardian* website.

SAVINGS AND PENSIONS – DOING WHAT'S RIGHT FOR YOU

Hopefully, with all the savings you're going to make, and all the information you now know how to access, you're going to turn your attention to saving for your future. If you don't already have a pension or savings, then work out how you can start putting money away. After all, you're probably going to be working in some capacity or other until you're about 70, so you've got time to make a real difference to your future if you begin now. It's never too late to save.

Lots of women hate the idea of locking their cash away in a pension. If this applies to you, invest in the kind of savings you feel comfortable with, such as National Savings Certificates. Once you begin to build up a bit of a nest egg, you may grow in confidence and become more adventurous.

If you want a pension, there are two main types:

1 The ones that you pay into where you work.
2 Pensions that you set up for yourself – or through a financial adviser.

Getting the right help

My suggestion is that you talk through your options with someone on the women's helpline at the Pensions Advisory Service. There's also good information and advice from the

Financial Services Authority (FSA). For example, if you're pondering how much money you have and how much you'll need for the future, the FSA has useful interactive calculation pages on the Money Made Clear part of their website.

If you decide you need a financial adviser, make sure she (or he) is registered with the FSA. You can check via the FSA website, or by ringing the Money Made Clear Helpline. Currently, most advisers will charge you about £225 per session, but many offer a free initial consultation. And some won't charge you if you have money to invest, because they'll get a commission from the company they put your money with.

However in 2012, the FSA is going to stop advisers getting a payout from financial institutions when they invest your money in savings plans. Personally, I think this is a good thing, because it's been hard to determine just how 'independent' some independent financial advisers have been. I imagine some of them will find it harder to survive without these commissions, so it's probably going to mean that the fees they charge us customers will become more competitive. At least that's my theory.

Take the best of three

Make sure when choosing a financial adviser that you can understand what he or she is telling you. Some of them speak in a jargon all their own. Financial expert Simonne Gnessen says that a woman should go for initial (and hopefully free) consultations with three different advisers before selecting the one she rates most.

Make a will

- Did you know that if you don't make a will, all sorts of appalling things could happen – like your ex could inherit all your money!

- Did you also know that if you die without making a will, the state takes 40 per cent of your assets before your nearest and dearest get a thing?

Dying intestate is crazy. I know that making a will is not the most palatable thing to have to do, but lots of us have complicated and extended families and stepfamilies – and we want to make sure that our money (if we have any) goes to the right people. So do make a will. You can do it through a solicitor, or get information on how to do it yourself on the Direct Gov website in the Government, Citizens and Rights section.

Alternatively, find a company called Law Pack online. They will sell you a DIY Will Kit for a tenner.

STATE STUFF

Finally, let's look at what we in the UK might get from the State. If you were born on or before 5 April 1950 you'll get your state pension at 60. Those born later will have to wait longer.

Your pensionable age

Between 2010 and 2020, the female retirement age will gradually increase until it reaches 65. Then, between 2024 and 2046 the retirement age for both genders will again rise bit by bit until it reaches 68.

You can check when you'll be able to draw your pension by going on to the Pension Service website and clicking on the heading State Pension Calculator. Currently, the state pension is £95.25 for a single person. A couple get £152.30. But the amount you're entitled to will be reduced if you haven't worked for enough 'qualifying years'.

Will you get a full state pension?

Unfortunately, while they were at home with their children, many female baby boomers chose to pay a reduced 'married woman stamp' rather than the full National Insurance contribution. This meant that even though they later returned to the workplace, they still didn't qualify for the full state pension because they hadn't paid a full stamp for a total of 39 years. However, in recent years, the government introduced a strategy whereby we could top up any missing contributions while we're still working, so that we'll get the full pension on retirement.

In 2010, there will be a further change in the rules, entitling women to a full pension if they have completed 30 years in work rather than the previous requirement of 39 years. This is going to make a tremendous difference to many of us. So if you've been thinking that you need to top up the years when you paid only the married woman's stamp, you may not need to. Check with the Pension Service website, or ring their helpline.

Are you due some credits?

From 2010, there's a new benefit called Carer's Credit. Basically, this will benefit women who may not have worked outside of the home, because they were full-time carers inside it for a child or an elderly person. Again, the Pension Service can give you more details.

They can also tell you about Pension Credits. If you're of pensionable age, and are finding it hard to manage, you might be eligible for an extra payment which will bring your weekly income from the State up to £124.05 if you're single, or £189.35 if you're part of a couple.

Still working past retirement age?

If you continue to work past retirement age, you can claim your pension at the same time. You won't have to pay any more National Insurance contributions though – so long as you've paid them in full for sufficient years – but you will have to pay tax. However, you can delay taking your pension if you don't need it.

For more information, phone the Pension Service, or go to their website and find the link for State Pension. When that page comes up, scroll down until you get to State Pension Deferral. Then click on What are My Choices at State Pension Age? As you'll see, if you put if off for long enough, you'll have several options, including the right to take out a lump sum. This will benefit you, if you can afford to do it.

WHERE TO FIND OUT MORE

Car Sharing: www.liftshare.com/uk
City Car Club: www.citycarclub.co.uk
Citizens' Advice Bureau (CAB): www.citizensadvice.co.uk
Direct Gov: www.direct.gov.uk
50 Connect: www.50connect.co.uk
Financial Services Authority (FSA): www.fsa.gov.uk
    Also: www.moneymadeclear.fsa.gov.uk; tel. 0300 500 5000
Guardian website: www.guardian.co.uk
Jasmine Birtles: www.moneymagpie.com
Lawpack: www.lawpack.co.uk
London Stock Exchange: www.londonstockexchange.com
Love Food Hate Waste: www.lovefoodhatewaste.com;
    tel. 0808 100 2040
Motley Fool: www.fool.co.uk
National Debtline: www.nationaldebtline.co.uk; tel. 0808
    808 4000
Pensions Advisory Service:
    www.pensionsadvisoryservice.org.uk
Pensions Advisory Service Women's helpline: tel. 0845 600
    0806
Pension Service: www.thepensionservice.gov.uk; tel. 0845
    606 0265 (general enquiries); 0800 99 1234 (to claim
    Pension Credit); 0800 731 7898 (to claim State Pension)
Rias: www.rias.co.uk
Dr Ros Altmann: www.rosaltmann.com
Saga: www.saga.co.uk
Simonne Gnessen: www.wise-monkey.org.uk;
    www.sheconomics.com
Unbiased: www.unbiased.co.uk

BOOKS

The Money Magpie: I Can Help You Ditch Your Debts, Make Money and Save £1000s, by Jasmine Birtles, published by Vermilion
Sheconomics, by Karen Pine and Simonne Gnessen, published by Headline

---

START NOW FOR A GOOD FUTURE

So, that's my whistle-stop tour through our financial situation. It's a total drag that the economy went pear-shaped just when we were relying on it. But, that's life! The important thing now is for us to get on top of what our own financial situation is. Most of us also need to start saving much more than we have been – so get that old piggy bank down from the loft.

If we become as solvent as possible, we'll have more of a chance to fulfil the exciting and innovative plans we have for our futures.

Can we do it? Yes we can!

CHAPTER 4

Feeling Absolutely Fabulous

'A bear, however hard he tries, grows tubby
without exercise.' (A. A. Milne)

I guess that most of us hope, and expect, to live longer than our parents, but longevity isn't all it's cracked up to be, unless you're fit enough to enjoy it. None of us can guarantee good health, but what we *can* do is keep ourselves in as good nick as possible by exercising and eating well.

So, this chapter is all about keeping active, and fuelling our bodies with nutritious food, so that we can feel 'absolutely fabulous', and have real quality of life as we get older. First, let's focus on exercise.

ARE WE ACTIVE ENOUGH?

Current government guidelines recommend that we do 30 minutes of moderate to vigorous exercise five days a week, but my own survey shows that only 16 per cent of us boomers are doing that.

Why is that? After all, we've seen our parents get slow and stiff and we know how awfully ageing that looks. Is that what we want for ourselves? No! We want to be lively and lissom and young-looking. Also, we want to be happy and optimistic, and many of us already know that exercise boosts the levels of endorphins, or 'happy chemicals', in our bloodstreams.

Not very keen on exercise

Unfortunately, despite knowing that exercise is good for us, lots of us aren't keen on it, and our lack of enthusiasm is often a legacy from our childhoods, when PE was frequently a source of dread to us girls. For a start it was undignified: prancing around in navy knickers didn't do much for our self-image! Also, in many schools in those days, if you had no natural sporting talent, you either got shouted at or ignored. So it was no wonder that many of us grew up hating sport, and deciding we were 'useless' at exercise.

This was certainly true of me. I was one of those kids who was always picked last by my classmates for the rounders team. So I gave up sport as soon as I could. And during my twenties and thirties, the only exercise I got was from lifting a glass or a cigarette to my lips, or having sex. But then I slowly began to change.

How I put my inactive past behind me

It was vanity that got me into exercise: bits of me were beginning to head south and I didn't like it. I can't now remember when that magical switch happened in my brain so that instead of thinking *I really ought to exercise*, I thought *I really want to exercise*. But once it did happen, it transformed my life – making me feel fitter and more energetic than I ever had before.

How did it happen though? Well, for one thing I picked forms of exercise that I wanted to try. I'd always fancied playing tennis, but thought I'd be hopeless. However, since my husband was keen to take it up too, I gave it a go. Initially, I was dreadful, but I liked how it engaged my brain so that I didn't notice I was running around – and gradually I improved.

Then I started going to a gym to use weights and machines to tone me up. That was a revelation, as I soon began to see how thighs can improve by using the adductor machine, how breasts lift through using the pec-deck, and how you keep those bingo-wings at bay by using dumb-bells.

It's time just for you

Another important factor for me was turning those gym visits into precious, personal time. This meant that instead of exercise being a chore, it became part of a whole experience that I looked forward to.

My gym is by the sea, and when I arrive I go straight to the coffee shop and have a cappuccino, then read a newspaper while looking out on the Channel, before I do the exercise. (By the way, coffee speeds up your metabolism, so if you drink it before you work out, rather than after, it increases the efficacy of your effort.)

I go three or four times a week, if I possibly can. Also, in the same building, the club offers a range of dance classes – so I've taken up ballet. I'd always longed to have ballet lessons as a child, but my mother wouldn't let me. She was keener on me having piano lessons. And she used to say, 'When you're 90 you won't be able to pirouette down the hall, but you'll still be able to sit at the piano and play a tune.' Well, it's now my intention to do both!

Ballet is fantastic for core strength – which is all about getting the muscles in your back stronger – and for improving coordination and balance. It also seems to reduce cellulite.

My gym costs me less than £70 monthly, and since I go so regularly, it works out at about a fiver per visit. For that money I can also do as many classes as I like. I could swim as well, if only I had the time to wash and dry my hair afterwards!

If I fall on hard times, I'll give up eating out, having holidays and haircuts before relinquishing my gym membership. Why? Because I really like how I feel when I'm fit.

———— **BABY-BOOMER FACT** ————

The oldest woman in the 2009 London Marathon was 80-year-old Doreen Offredi – and she didn't even take up running until she was 58!

Finding your motivation

So, would you like to feel healthier, stronger and more energetic? Most of us would. Most of us too – being intelligent women – know that exercise is a good route to feeling fabulously fit. And yet, few of us do nearly enough.

I reckon that this is because we haven't truly grasped how fantastic we're going to feel, and so we're not motivated enough. As I found, once you're able to make your exercise regime into something you look forward to – and to keep at it till you feel great – then motivation is no problem. But until you do, it can be hard going.

So, the important thing is to work out how you can get motivated to start exercising more – and to do that you need to engage your mind.

Get the mindset

One way to do this might be to identify something specific that you can't do at the moment, but which you could do if you were fitter. Would you like to:

- Be able to run round the park with your grandson?
- Be able to walk up the stairs without feeling puffed?
- Look and feel more toned for yourself, or your lover?
- Feel more alert in your mind, and less exhausted in your body?

Well, taking up regular exercise could help you to achieve all of the above. Would that be sufficient motivation to get you started?

Or has there perhaps been a sad event that could be a trigger for you to get active? Sometimes a friend – or a parent – dying of cancer can be all the motivation we need to train for a fund-raising event such as the Race for Life.

We can find motivation in many different ways. What will do it for you?

How to keep motivated

Once you've found your motivation to get started, the next stage is to maintain your enthusiasm, and you'll only do that if you pick a form of exercise that you like. It would be pointless to take up swimming if you find it boring as hell, and if you have an aversion to gyms – and all those sweaty blokes grunting and straining under their weights – then that's probably not going to work for you either.

How exercise has changed

Very few baby boomers went to school by car. Mostly we walked. So we started and ended the day with exercise.

Our mums didn't go to the gym – they did all their own housework instead – and back in the 1950s and 1960s that was a much more back-breaking activity than it is today.

However, some mothers did do Health and Beauty. Maybe you recall fuzzy TV pictures of Eileen Fowler putting matronly women through very ladylike and gentle physical jerks. What would they have made of today's jazz ballet, aerobic classes or boot camps?

However, perhaps you would join a fitness centre where there was a women-only gym, and where they have the televisions tuned to property programmes, *This Morning* and re-runs of *Midsomer Murders* rather than wall-to-wall sport!

Go green

If indoor gyms are never going to be your thing, perhaps you'd enjoy exercising at an outdoor or 'green' gym? These are actually conservation projects that combine energetic physical activity with doing something useful for the environment. If you'd like getting together with similarly minded people, and exercising in the open air, this could be ideal. You can get more details from BTCV (British Trust for Conservation Volunteers).

The fun factor

Exercise should be fun – and when it is, it's easy to keep motivated. TV pundit Tina Baker, who is also a qualified fitness instructor, thinks that dancing around the house is a great way to get fit. She says: 'Put on some dance music that you like and start slowly by swaying and walking on the spot, so that you warm up your muscles. Then, get more active. Punch your arms above your head. March up and down. Jump. Whatever feels good.'

You might like dancing at home so much that you'll opt to sign up for a dance class. What about Salsa? Tap? Ceroc? Ballroom? Dancing elevates your mood, and it also improves bone density, balance, flexibility, coordination and posture.

Are you feeling motivated and inspired yet? If not, what about belly dancing – a friend of mine does it and she says it's a huge laugh and that her body is now in better shape than it was in her twenties!

Or why not consider aqua aerobics, kick boxing, or tae kwon do? Or badminton, golf or rollerblading? And how about cycling – especially now there are so many cycle lanes and paths? If you're on an economy drive and thinking of giving up your car, getting a bike could provide transport and activity in one neat package.

Then there is Pilates, yoga, or Alexander Technique classes – all of which are great for strengthening back muscles and for toning and flexibility.

Walk to good health

Don't forget walking – it's great for fitness: a good pair of shoes and an open space, and you're away! Walking is sociable too. Masses of people who go on organised walks find friendship and romance. Ramblers (formerly The Ramblers' Association) is great to join. Or get inspired by fitness guru Joanna Hall's website and her Walk Active Programme.

The family factor

Finally, could you find motivation to get active with your grandchildren? Perhaps you could play football in the park, or if you're a really 'cool' granny, you could exercise with them using a Wii console. Unlike most video games you participate by actually moving your body and arms as you play whatever sport is on the screen. It certainly looks like fun.

Quick fixes are in short supply!

Being all too human, we can get disheartened and find that our motivation flags if our exercise regime doesn't result in a 'quick fix'. In truth, we'd like to be transformed into Madonna overnight – even if we look like Dawn French to begin with! But don't be tempted to do too much too soon.

Start slowly – and for short periods of time – until you get stronger. Far too many people go crazy and do a ten-mile walk, or a two-hour gym session, on the first day they start to exercise. Not surprisingly, they hurt themselves and are put off for life.

Getting into the habit of exercising can be hard. And you might start with enthusiasm, but become fed up if the results aren't spectacular – and then start thinking you've got other things to do or that you'd sooner read a book. When that happens:

- Vary your exercise routine so that the same muscles aren't being used – or becoming sore – all the time, and you're not getting bored.
- Get a friend to join your fitness regime – you can motivate each other to keep going.
- If, in the past, you used to exercise a lot – maybe you used to 'go for the burn' along with Jane Fonda – cast your mind back to how marvellous it felt to be fit.

Watch the changes

Another way to motivate yourself is to recognise the small changes that are beginning to happen. After just a couple of weeks, you should notice that bits of your body are firmer than before, and that you're less breathless, or that you feel happy after exercising. Small changes build into big benefits, if you keep at it.

Weight loss

What if you're looking to lose weight through exercise? Unfortunately, there is no guarantee that exercise alone will take off the pounds. But what *will* happen is that your clothes will feel looser and you'll start liking your body more. You'll probably find you begin being more choosy about the sort of food you're prepared to put into the 'new, improved' you – and you'll develop a genuine interest in eating more healthily, which will lead to weight loss.

Having said that, fitness guru Joanna Hall makes great claims on her website about how much weight women can lose just through walking, so you might want to read the advice on her Walk Active programme as mentioned above.

Get super-active

Another form of exercise, which is almost certain to get the pounds dropping off you, is a boot camp. The term 'boot camp' was originally used to describe a camp for training recruits to the US Marine Corps. It was tough! Nowadays a boot camp tends to mean a period of intensive supervised physical activity based on military principles. Personally, I don't think you should try this if you're an exercise novice, but if you've been active for a while, and are keen to lose some weight, a boot camp could be just the thing. My friend and fellow health journalist Patsy Westcott recently went on one. She lost 1.8kg (4lb) and 'several inches off several places!' And she looks amazing.

New year – new challenge

Once you're more active than you were, you'll probably start to get all sorts of ideas about tackling new types of exercise. I think it's a good idea to review your exercise programme annually – perhaps at New Year. We're far too young to start winding down – instead I suggest that we add something new to our fitness menu every year. That should keep the rocking chair at bay!

HOW FOOD HAS CHANGED

Now, let's turn our attention to eating. Can you imagine what your seven-year-old self would have made of today's supermarkets, or greengrocers, or nearest deli – let alone the food hall in Selfridges? She'd have been blown away by just how much food has changed since our childhoods.

One small example of that is olive oil, which our mums bought only for medicinal purposes from chemists. They used to rub it on their faces, or put some on a warmed spoon and drip it into our ears when we had earache. In Britain, no one cooked with it. So who'd have thought that it would become a staple in today's healthy eating plans?

Feel-good foods

Back in our childhoods I think that many mothers were too busy making ends meet to worry much about healthy eating. But today is different and we've never had a better chance to feel good through the food that we eat. Unfortunately, however, many of us have the idea that 'feel-good foods' are those that give us a sugar rush or a comfort-fix; for example, buns, pizzas, biscuits, chocolate and fizzy drinks. The truth is that these only give us a short-term burst of energy – and after it's over we usually feel stodgy, bloated and tired. Unfortunately, though, they can be quite addictive, so we keep going back to them.

We need, therefore, to find different feel-good foods: foods that are healthy and which genuinely make us feel good – in our bodies and in our minds.

When I see clients who are depressed, or very stressed, I usually find that their diets are diabolical. Many of them skip breakfast, overdose on coffee and sugary snacks, grab a sandwich – which they eat at their desks at lunchtime – and pick up a ready-meal and too much booze at the end of the day. These are intelligent people, but they're treating their bodies appallingly. No wonder they're in such a state.

I get them to alter their diets by:

1 Eating breakfast (usually porridge).
2 Having healthy snacks, such as fruit, nuts or seeds.
3 Substituting salad and protein for their usual lunchtime sandwich.
4 Reducing their alcohol intake.

5 Eating a nutritious supper of lightly grilled fish or poultry and fresh vegetables.

And what happens? They soon feel much more in control of their emotions, and they have more energy.

Super-foods

Real 'feel-good' foods — those that genuinely give us energy and help us feel fit and well — include the ones now often referred to as 'super-foods'. Here's a list of them:

apples	peaches
beetroot	plums
blackberries	raspberries
blueberries	red grapes
Brazil nuts	red onions
broccoli	rocket
cherries	salmon
cranberries	spinach
garlic	strawberries
green tea	sweet potatoes
olive oil	tomatoes
oranges	

There isn't a scientific definition of a super-food, but many dieticians and nutritionists believe that these foods are rich in good nutrients and offer protection against heart disease and cancer.

Our generation was the first to . . .

. . . cook differently from our mothers. It wasn't just clothes and music that altered in our teens and early adulthood, there was a lot more interesting and varied food around too, so cooking was more fun. Recipe books became colourful and user-friendly. And TV cooks grew jollier – out went Fanny Craddock and in came The Galloping Gourmet. And there was the *Cordon Bleu Cookery Course* in 'part-work' form too.

We're still learning, and these days there are plenty of books on healthy styles of cooking so that we can enjoy food and keep well nourished and fit.

Healthy ways of eating

There are plenty of super-foods in the kind of healthy-eating plans that nutritionists recommend – the Mediterranean Diet, for example.

Fresh and sunny

The Mediterranean Diet has been lauded for years as a route to healthier living. People who live in some parts of the Mediterranean – such as Greece, Italy and the South of France – eat plenty of fish, and they cook in olive oil as well as sprinkling it on salads. They also eat loads of fresh fruit and vegetables. What they don't eat are processed foods, butter and other saturated fats – or as much red meat as the average Briton or American. And they tend to live longer than us.

Lower cholesterol and all-round good health

Recently, a new healthy-eating plan, called the Portfolio Diet, has appeared on the scene, and many dieticians recommend it. It's similar to the Mediterranean Diet, but it has some extra ingredients, which include cholesterol-lowering substances called plant stanols or sterols. You've probably seen yogurt drinks, fruit juices and spreads that say they are fortified with plant sterols or stanols. If you follow the Portfolio Diet you'll be encouraged to include such items daily.

The diet also urges you to eat 23 almonds a day – although I haven't been able to find out why that is such a precise figure! You're also encouraged to consume plenty of porridge oats and soya protein – which can be in the form of soya milk, soya yogurts, beans or tofu. It's claimed that following this plan can reduce your cholesterol levels by 25 per cent. For more information, go to the Heart UK website.

Whether or not you need to lower your cholesterol, the Portfolio Diet is a healthy way to eat, and it will almost certainly boost your energy levels and leave you feeling satisfied, and never stodgy.

Eat good fats

Probably the most vital message for us baby boomers is that we should eat good fats (unsaturated) as opposed to bad (saturated) ones. If we don't cut down on saturated fats, we won't feel energetic for much longer, because our arteries will get more and more clogged up – and we'll be at risk of serious heart disease, or death.

Top dietician Sian Porter says that in the UK, saturated

fat comprises over 13 per cent of the average person's diet and that the most we should have is 10 per cent. Sian is one of the experts on The Fat Panel, which is a group of dieticians and doctors who provide objective information on the important role of oils and fats in the diet. Recently they produced some useful tips for reducing saturated fat in our diets:

1 **Limit consumption of butter**, lard and ghee, as these are rich sources of saturated fat. Replace with small amounts of unsaturated fats such as rapeseed oil, olive oil, sunflower oil, or spreads made from these.

2 **Choose lean cuts** of meat and trim off any visible fat. Have chicken or turkey without the skin. Cut right back on processed meats such as spam, salami and corned beef, and meat pies, sausage rolls and breaded meat or chicken.

3 **Add less meat** to stews and casseroles, and replace with vegetables, beans and pulses, such as lentils.

4 **Read labels** on food products so that you can choose those with less saturated fat.

5 **Have pies with only one crust** rather than two – either a lid or a base – because pastry is very high in fat.

6 **Use spreads** instead of butter. This can substantially reduce the saturated fat you are eating. For example, a 10g portion of typical sunflower oil margarine contains 1.2g saturated fat, compared to 5.4g in the same-size portion of butter.

7 **Choose lower-fat versions** of dairy produce, such as skimmed, or semi-skimmed milk, reduced-fat yogurt, and lower fat cheeses (such as cottage cheese and 0 per cent fat fromage frais).

Eat local – eat well

One criticism of the kind of feel-good, healthy eating I'm suggesting is that it costs a lot compared to ordinary super-market fare. Well, it's true that some feel-good foods are expensive, but if you shop for your meals daily, from local suppliers, and buy only what you want for that day, you'll cut out loads of waste. When we go to the supermarket and indulge in lots of BOGOF (buy one, get one free) foods, most of us end up throwing lots of it away.

Grow your own

You can really get into healthy eating by growing some of your own food. A delightful book called *The Virgin Gardener*, by Laetitia Maklouf, will tell you how – even if you've never done it before, or think you don't have the space to try.

One great bonus of growing older is that we often have more time to shop and to cook fresh food from scratch. And we don't have the complications in the home that we did when we were trying to feed a whole family. Let's face it, many mums end up cooking five different meals for five different, and fussy, individuals. Once our kids have flown the nest, we can stop all that nonsense. So, we can buy little and often – and get it locally from butchers, fishmongers and greengrocers we trust. Also, we'll be doing our bit to combat global warming, as locally sourced food is not only reckoned to be more nutritious but also has a low carbon footprint.

THE GREAT WATER DEBATE

We can also reduce food miles by foregoing mineral water and drinking tap water instead – and talking of water, how much should we be drinking?

Now, we probably all know that we should drink enough fluid to keep hydrated – and that the usual health recommendation is that we need to consume eight glasses of water a day.

However, in 2008, two scientists from the University of Pennsylvania questioned whether we need to drink this much at all. In fact, they said they couldn't even find out where the 'eight glasses of water daily' message had first started.

So, what should we do? Well, I think that most of us do actually feel better – and I believe that our skin looks better too – if we drink the recommended eight glasses a day, especially in hot weather. I also think that drinking sufficient water helps us with bladder problems. Unfortunately, as we get older, some of us get recurring cystitis, or a feeling of 'urgency' that can make us feel very insecure when we're out and don't know where the nearest loo is. If we drink sufficient water, our urine becomes dilute and takes on a pale straw colour, which is healthier for the bladder. So why not let the colour of your pee be your guide as to how much water you need?

Coffee and tea, by the way, contain mild diuretics – called methylxanthines – and can make that sense of urgency worse.

YOU AND YOUR TIPPLE

I never saw either of my grandmothers drink alcohol. And certainly women of their generation never went into pubs – unless accompanied by a male. I doubt if many of our mothers went to pubs on their own either, or even in the company of other women. How different we have been! Booze has been a big part of our social lives – and we've enjoyed it.

But does it still help us feel good? Well actually, I can't have more than a glass of wine these days without feeling sluggish, headachey and a bit vague – and I know I'm not alone. However, there are plenty of baby boomers who can still drink their partners under the table – and we've probably all been to birthday parties for 50- or 60-year-olds that have been loud and riotous affairs. I remember one where the daughter of the birthday girl took her mum to one side and told her off for being so uproarious. There's plenty of partying in us yet!

Happy hours

Getting boozed occasionally is one thing; however, routine, daily drinking is quite another. Lots of women who spend more time in their own home as they get older find that 'happy hour' is starting earlier and earlier, and as a result they're sinking large amounts of alcohol daily.

As Dr Tom Smith wrote in his *Guardian* column recently, 'A bottle of wine a day puts a woman at high risk of liver and brain disease.' So, if we want to continue to feel fabulously fit and well, we really should confine ourselves to 14 units of alcohol a week.

DO WE NEED SUPPLEMENTS TO MAKE US FEEL GOOD?

Many doctors and dieticians firmly believe that if we eat a healthy diet, we don't need to take any supplements. I have to confess that I used to be a supplement junkie, but even I have come to the opinion that it's best to get all your essential vitamins and minerals through a healthy diet rather than from a pill bottle. The Food Standards Agency website, and the website of the British Dietetic Association, both have excellent information on this subject.

I guess that most of us know how to get plenty of vitamin C from food, but I think we can be a bit unsure about some of the other vitamins – particularly vitamins D and K, which nutritionists tell us we must have as we get older.

- **Vitamin D** is essential for our bones. We get some of this from sunlight. Oily fish is another good source.

- **Vitamin K** is also essential for our bones and our longevity. It's mainly found in green vegetables like broccoli and spinach.

We also need appropriate amounts of certain minerals. Three of the most important are calcium, iron and potassium:

- **Calcium** Women of our age should be getting 1,200mg of calcium daily. There's about 750mg of calcium in a pint of milk, so if you use that much in tea, coffee and on your cereal every day, you're on your way to getting enough. Other good sources are in butter, cheese and other dairy products. But if you're watching your consumption of those types of food because of your weight or cholesterol, you need to bump up your calcium intake another way. You can get calcium from soya beans, soya milk, tofu, chickpeas, green vegetables like watercress and cabbage, dried fruits – especially dried figs – and Brazil nuts. And do remember that there's as much calcium in skimmed milk as there is in the full-cream variety.

- **Iron** There's no doubt that because many of us eat little red meat – for health reasons – we may be deficient in iron, especially if we're vegans or vegetarians. Women over 50 still need 8.7mg of iron per day. If you're not getting enough, you'll feel tired all the time and you might be anaemic. Iron is easy to take as a supplement. But there are good sources of it in our food – particularly in liver, red meat, canned sardines, beans, nuts, dried fruit (especially dried apricots), fortified breakfast cereals and some green leafy vegetables.

- **Potassium** is another essential mineral for the function of the cells of the body. In the UK, we're advised to consume 3,500mg of it a day, but in America the recommendation is 4,700mg. Just to give you an idea, one banana has only about 400mg of potassium in it. So you need to include other good sources of this mineral, which include potato, sweet potato, yogurt, some oily fish, cod, beef, spinach, citrus fruits and dried apricots.

If you want to read a good book on nutrition – including lots of well-researched information on supplements – I suggest you buy Patrick Holford's *New Optimum Nutrition Bible*.

GOOD HABITS TO HELP YOU LOSE WEIGHT

It's hard to feel really fabulously fit and well if you're fatter than you'd like to be – and I'm afraid that lots of us baby boomers are. To be honest, I'd always assumed that those of us aged between 45 and 65 were less likely to be lardy than younger people – mainly because we were reared before the days of fast food. But when I checked the statistics with the NHS Information Centre, I found that a staggering 69 per cent of us are regarded as being 'overweight'.

This contrasts sharply with our neighbours across the channel. The Body Mass Index (BMI) of the average French woman is 23.2, which falls into the 'ideal range' of between 18.5 and 25. The typical UK woman's BMI is 26.2, which is 'overweight'.

So, why are we fatter? Is it because French women care more about their appearance? Or is it because they've traditionally done what we're just beginning to do – which is to shop daily from local suppliers and to cook from scratch? Whatever it is, it's working. To get an insight into how the French think, shop and eat, do read the best-selling book *French Women Don't Get Fat* by Mireille Guiliano.

Frankly, if you're keen to lose weight, the best thing to do is to adopt some healthy lifestyle habits – rather than putting yourself on 'a diet'.

I love my body just the way it is, I love my bulgy belly, I love my . . .

oh forget it

Fat round the middle

A great book to help baby boomers lose that stubborn extra weight that is so reluctant to shift around our waists is Marilyn Glenville's *Fat Around the Middle*. Her website is great too.

Good things you can do are to:

1 **Eat regularly.** Aim to have breakfast, a mid-morning snack, lunch, a mid-afternoon snack and dinner, spaced at regular intervals. Never go for longer than four hours without consuming something – except overnight – but try not to eat at other times.

2 **Never go shopping when you're hungry** – you'll end up buying loads of stuff that will sabotage your plan to get slimmer.

3 **Designate two places only for eating** in your house – perhaps the dining table and kitchen bar or table. Forbid yourself food anywhere else. This means no standing at the fridge door and snacking on leftovers, and pretending you're not really eating!

4 **Identify some foods that you can do without** – and which are packed full of saturated fats and sugar – and then refuse to buy them. If you can outlaw biscuits, pizza and cakes from the house, you won't binge or snack on them.

5 **Never starve yourself.** You'll only end up bingeing later.

6 **Eat colourful and nutritious foods**. Always have a portion of something red, orange or purple, and another of something green, with every meal.

7 **Focus on a meal when you're eating it**. Chew slowly and don't read a book or watch the TV at the same time.

What not to do if you're trying to shed the pounds

If you can encourage good habits and a real respect for healthy food, you'll be less inclined to fill up on the kind of rubbish that makes you heavy. At the same time you need to avoid items that perhaps you've always resorted to in the past:

1 **Diet drinks and artificial sweeteners**. Ask yourself this: has the population of the Western world grown thinner because of all the dietary foods we can now buy? The answer of course is no. In fact, Professor Kelly Brownell of Yale University says that using artificial sweeteners can cause people to eat more. He says that a sweet taste on the tongue brings about an expectation in the brain of a certain amount of calories, and that when the body doesn't receive those calories it compensates by eating more. So don't buy yourself diet drinks or dietary meals. They're a waste of money.

2 **Meal replacements**. Avoid any diet that involves 'meal replacement'. This kind of diet system doesn't educate you to enjoy eating appropriate amounts of

good, nutritious food. Instead, it transports you to some weird kind of limbo land where you don't eat normally at all, and all you can think about is your next milkshake or fibre bar.

I'm not saying these diets don't get results. They often do in the short-term, but all the women I know who have gone on them have ballooned in weight as soon as they've stopped the plan and gone back to eating real food. And they've all ended up bigger than when they started.

And here's the golden rule. No matter how much you want to lose weight, **never skip breakfast.** Your tummy needs some food in it to give your body and mind enough energy to get going each morning. And don't delude yourself into thinking that a latte on the way to work will do.

Did you know . . .

. . . that drinks are no substitute for food? Professor Brownell says that they don't fill us up in the same way as solid food. So if we have a drink that provides 200 calories, we don't tend to feel as satisfied as we do if we eat solid food of the same caloric value – which means we often end up eating more in the long run.

Don't use food to sort your moods

Some of the most obese patients I've seen have been very knowledgeable about Weight Watchers points, or GI indices, or calorific values. One woman even insisted on finding out how many calories there are in the male ejaculate. This added a fresh dimension to the old oral-sex debate about whether or not to swallow!

But all this information frequently fails to result in weight loss. Why is that? Well, it's usually because, for all their knowledge, these patients go on binges that are nothing to do with genuine hunger or fuelling their bodies.

Does this sound like you? If so, keep a diary of when you overeat things you're trying to avoid, and then ask yourself what you were thinking about just before you started eating. Perhaps you were thinking:

- I need cheering up.
- I deserve a treat.
- I have to have it, because I had a difficult day.

These thoughts are likely to create a mood that is not a comfortable one, such as feeling unloved, or bored, or angry, or irritated. Unfortunately, it's really common for us to go scurrying to the cookie jar when we get those moods – in an attempt to escape them, and find some comfort.

Inevitably, this form of comfort sabotages all efforts to get slim and healthy. Worse than that, it's incredibly short-lived. If I ask a client how long the comfort went on, she'll probably admit that it only lasted seconds: just while the chocolate or other treat was actually in her mouth. As soon as she swallowed it, the comfort disappeared and was replaced by guilt and loathing.

So, use your mind to identify feelings and thoughts – and to find ways other than food for dealing with them. You could:

- Take a scented bath surrounded by candles.
- Play soothing music.
- Ring a friend or sibling.
- Put on a DVD that you've been meaning to watch.

Food shouldn't be used to solve moods. We need to deal with our feelings in other ways.

WHERE TO FIND OUT MORE

EXERCISE

Adventure Boot Camps: www.fitnesscamp.co.uk
Brighton Boot Camp: www.brightonbootcamp.com
Green gyms: www2.btcv.org.uk/display/greengym
Joanna Hall: www.joannahall.com
New You Boot Camps: www.newyoubootcamp.com
Ramblers: www.ramblers.org.uk
Tina Baker: http://web.me.com/tinabaker

EATING

British Dietetic Association (BDA): www.bda.uk.com
Food Standards Agency: www.eatwell.gov.uk

Heart UK: www.heartuk.org.uk
Marilyn Glenville: www.marilynglenville.com
NHS Information Centre www.ic.nhs.uk

BOOKS

New Optimum Nutrition Bible, by Patrick Holford, published by
Piatkus

The Virgin Gardener, by Laetitia Maklouf, published by
Bloomsbury

French Women Don't Get Fat, by Mireille Guiliano, published by
Chatto and Windus

Fat Around the Middle, by Marilyn Glenville, published by Kyle
Cathie

FOOD IS SOMETHING TO ENJOY NOT MISUSE

There's been a lot of information to absorb in this chapter, but I hope that it will inspire you to motivate yourself to get active and to eat as healthily as you can, so that you'll soon feel absolutely fit and utterly fabulous.

CHAPTER 5

All in the Mind

'When it comes to staying young, a mind-lift beats a face-lift any day.' (Marty Bucella)

In the last chapter I focused on how we could feel better through exercising, and eating healthily. And some of what we discussed there will crop up again in this chapter, which is all about our minds – and how utterly fascinating they are!

I am passionate about good mental health for two main reasons. One is that when you have it, you can cope with virtually anything life throws at you. The other reason is that it's becoming increasingly obvious that if we take more responsibility for our own happiness, we can make ourselves much more mentally healthy. I find this really exciting.

We baby boomers have dealt with more changes and challenges than any generation before us. However, we can't exactly know what the demands of the next decades will be – but I believe that the more we've got our minds sorted, the better we'll cope.

MOTHERS' LITTLE HELPERS

Luckily for us, there are far more mental health options now than there were for our mothers. You might remember the Rolling Stones' song of 1966, 'Mother's Little Helper'. 'Mother's little helpers' were tranquillisers – like Valium – which were regarded as lifesavers by some of our mums, who didn't know then how addictive these pills were.

Some of us as children remember our poor mothers having what used to be called 'trouble with their nerves'. Sadly, at that time, there was little help available to them except pharmaceutical treatment.

Not all of them thought that was a solution. My own mother hated the fact that when she went to see the GP, he reached for his prescription pad before she'd even opened her mouth! What she wanted was to talk and to be listened to, but there were no 'talking therapies' available then, unless you had money to go to a private analyst. So, what were doctors to do? The little 'yellow pill' that blurred the edges of tension or frustration was the best remedy they had.

In time, doctors stopped dishing out tranquillisers as if they were Smarties. But in the late 1980s, new types of antidepressants came on to the scene and they started prescribing them in prodigious quantities instead. These medications – the most famous being Prozac – were heralded as 'wonder drugs.' In fact, you might remember that loads of journalists at the time wrote articles suggesting that we should all be popping these 'feel-good' pills because they were just so great.

More than two decades on, we're beginning to look at good mental health in very many different ways – and thank heavens for that!

Change of language – and approach

Nowadays we use very different language when talking about our feelings. We say we're 'stressed out', 'phobic', or have 'low self-esteem'.

When we were young, almost any emotional upset was put down to 'your nerves'. And if a child was frequently distressed, she was known as 'a sensitive child'. And what was the usual parental advice? 'Pull yourself together'!

THE TIMES THEY ARE A-CHANGING

Numerous studies in recent years have shown that there are other, and often more effective, ways to help people to be more mentally healthy than simply taking pills. In fact, in 2008 Professor Irving Kirsch of Hull University published research showing that many patients improved almost as well on placebo (that is, fake medicine) as they did on antidepressants. He also revealed that many clinical trials had failed to show any benefits of drugs over placebo – and that these trials had frequently been withheld from publication.

His report caused a bit of a furore, I can tell you.

Being positive

Another development in mental health has been the emergence of the Positive Psychology movement. Its founder, Martin Seligman, decided that something must be wrong with mental health services that merely reacted to mental *illness* and did nothing to promote mental *health*.

He and his followers have been on a mission since the early 1990s to promote positive mental health by helping people to focus on their positive traits and emotions rather than on all their problems.

Most of this work is being done in America – and Positive Psychology is certainly not available in Britain on the NHS – but I have found it fascinating to read some of Seligman's books and to visit his Authentic Happiness website, and you might too.

Talking it through

Back in the UK, 'talking therapies' are at last becoming more available to people who are mentally distressed, instead of drugs being almost the only option. In fact, the British government has poured masses of money into improved access for such therapies – notably cognitive behaviour therapy, or CBT.

I admit to some bias here, as I'm a CBT therapist, but this kind of therapy makes really good sense and gives people the tools to help themselves. CBT is derived from the work of a Stoic philosopher called Epictetus, who believed: 'It's not things that upset us, but our view of things.' CBT teaches us to examine recurring negative thoughts – and also the unhelpful assumptions that we often jump to – and to challenge them and learn to re-think them more rationally.

Personally, I'd love to see the theory of CBT taught in schools, but I don't think this will ever happen. However, there are lots of good self-help books, which get individuals thinking in more logical ways, and I've put details of a few of them at the end of this chapter.

Prevention first

Another development is that we're beginning to look at mental health in a more holistic fashion. Just as the medical profession has been encouraging us in recent years to prevent physical illness by exercising and eating five servings of fruit and veg a day, mental health experts are now also beginning to focus on prevention.

COMMON-SENSE TACTICS

I know that many of us fear mental deterioration and depression in later life. But research is emerging that if we eat healthily, and do enough exercise, then not only will we feel good and improve our physical health but our brains will benefit too. One of the illnesses we definitely want to avoid as we get older is vascular dementia, which is a form of cognitive deterioration that often occurs after people have a stroke, or if they have high blood pressure, high cholesterol, diabetes or heart problems.

Psychiatrist and *Daily Telegraph* columnist Dr Max

Pemberton says that the best ways to avoid vascular dementia are to:

1 Keep your weight down.
2 Keep your cholesterol level down.
3 Keep your blood pressure down.
4 Be active.
5 Don't smoke.
6 Take a low-dose aspirin daily, if your doctor agrees.

So, it's good common sense to eat healthily and exercise regularly, not only for our physical health but for our mental health too.

Think youthfully

Attitude is everything. So from today, vow never to say:

'I'm too old to change now.'
'Oh-oh, senior moment!'
'I can't possibly grasp that at my age.'
'My memory's not what it was.'

When you utter these phrases, you not only send out a message to other people that you're slowing down and knocking on a bit but you also send the same signal to your own brain. What you need to do instead is encourage it to work harder!

Another common-sense thing we can do is to refuse to accept that serious mental decline is inevitable as we grow older. I know we're not likely to be as alert as we were when we were 25, but there are plenty of women older than us who are learning new skills, taking university degrees and continuing to work at what they enjoy. What's the difference between them and the rest of us? It's their attitude: they've decided that they're far too young to get old!

WHAT'S NEW IN SCIENCE?

Until recently, science wouldn't have been on your side if you'd taken it into your head to improve your brain function in mid life, rather than let it slide into decline. You see, scientists thought that once the brain was fully formed in early adulthood it couldn't continue to grow and develop. But in 1998, researchers discovered that new neurons (nerve cells) are continually being generated in the adult brain – and this means that we can carry on learning and remembering new things.

This has great implications for us. And there's further good news in that we can increase the growth of new neurons by exercising regularly.

Brain building

This is one of the main themes of a fascinating book called *Spark!* by Dr John Ratey of Harvard Medical School. He explains that the more physical exercise you do, the more your brain builds up amounts of a kind of protein called brain-derived neurotrophic factor, or BDNF. This substance feeds the neurons in our brains like a fertiliser nourishes plants – and it enables them to become more active, and to develop and grow. As a result, the brain is able to remember more things.

There are various studies in the book to support this theory. In one of them, 59 sedentary individuals aged 60–79 were given MRI scans to establish the condition of their brains. They were then divided into two groups. One lot were assigned to exercise on a treadmill for an hour, three times a week. The other bunch went on to a programme where they did only a bit of gentle stretching.

After six months, the people who had exercised on the treadmill were fitter than the other group, which you'd expect. But, astonishingly, when their brains were re-scanned, these people also had an increase in volume in the frontal and temporal lobes of the brain. Dr Ratey said: 'It remains to be seen if this work can be replicated, but the idea that just six months of exercise remodels these crucial areas of the brain is incredibly heartening. In the scans, the exercisers' brains looked as if they were two to three years younger than they were.'

I don't know about you, but this research makes me more determined than ever to keep exercising.

Beating depression

There are also studies in Dr Ratey's book showing that physical activity is a great antidote to depression – and more effective long term than medication. This is incredibly important for us as a generation, because we like common-sense remedies. We're also more suspicious and sceptical about medicines than our parents ever were, and we don't want to sink into a depressive decline – because we've got a whole lot of living to do yet.

STRAIGHT FROM THE SPECIALIST'S MOUTH

In my survey, a massive 64 per cent of female baby boomers said that they were seriously worried at the thought of 'losing their minds'. This isn't surprising since many of us have seen a parent disintegrate before our eyes with Alzheimer's. My own mother had this condition, and for years at the end of her life she didn't know who she was – let alone who anyone else was. It was a horrible and undignified end, and I know that many of you reading this book have had similarly awful experiences within your own family. So I contacted psychiatrist and dementia specialist Dr Gianetta Rands and asked her, as someone who is seeing people with Alzheimer's every day of her working life, what she thought we could do to avoid getting it.

Like psychiatrist Dr Pemberton, she urged us to keep physically healthy:

1 She said: 'Eat nutritiously, take regular moderate exercise, avoid extremes of weight (over and under), don't smoke, and only drink alcohol in small amounts.'
2 Also, it's crucial to 'reduce risks of, and improve control of, hypertension, diabetes, obesity, heart and artery disease, stroke and high cholesterol.'
3 'There's also good evidence that keeping the mind

active is beneficial in maintaining its function whether or not someone has dementia. There is research about the benefits of "cognitive stimulation" and social interaction in maintaining and improving cognitive abilities.'

4 She also told me that we should keep medication to a minimum – particularly sleeping tablets and other sedative drugs.

Your personal needs are important

Dr Rands is a firm believer in us focusing not only on our cognitive abilities but also on our emotional needs – including meaningful personal relationships with partners, friends and family. 'Spiritual needs are important too', she said. 'These will not necessarily be in the form of a formal or shared religion but more to do with believing in the relevance, value and meaning of one's activities and life.'

I don't know about you, but it gives me a lot of hope that, as a generation, we can do various sensible things that might keep Alzheimer's at bay rather than succumb to it as many of our older relatives have.

It's true that over the last 15 years, various drugs have been developed which seem to halt the rate of decline, or to improve symptoms, in Alzheimer's patients. But, so far, there is no actual cure – so, prevention must be our best bet of staying sane and sharp as we get older.

> *If it's good for your body,*
> *it's good for your brain*
>
> In an article for *Science Daily* in 2008, UCLA professor of neurology and science, Fernando Gómez-Pinilla, wrote: 'Diet, exercise and sleep have the potential to alter our brain health and mental function. This raises the exciting possibility that changes in diet are a viable strategy for enhancing cognitive abilities, protecting the brain from damage and counteracting the effects of aging.'

USE IT OR LOSE IT

Gianetta Rands mentioned 'cognitive stimulation' and, apart from exercise, this is probably the best way to keep our brains in shape. Brain boosting has become big business. In recent years, lots of pocket-sized electronic brain-games machines have flooded the market. There are also brain-enhancing programmes you can buy to use on your computer – including one called 'Mind Fit' which was launched by Professor of Synaptic Pharmacology, Baroness Susan Greenfield.

Not all clinicians agree that brain trainers do what they claim. But they're fun, and I suppose the truth is that even if they don't do us much good, they certainly won't do us harm. However, you don't have to go 'electronic' if you want to keep your brain in good nick.

Can coffee cure Alzheimer's?

In July 2009, there was a flurry of headlines claiming that coffee could cure Alzheimer's. In reality, all that's happened so far is that some experiments on cognitively impaired mice have shown that caffeine improves their memory. Hopefully, in time, this research may have real relevance for us. But at the moment it's only good news if you're a forgetful mouse who likes coffee!

A new thing a day ...

One tactic many psychologists recommend is to do new and challenging things every day. And also to do familiar activities in non-familiar ways – such as tackling the ironing with the wrong hand, or reading a newspaper that you'd normally find too intellectual or dull, or tackling a sudoku instead of a crossword.

Making music

Music is also reckoned to be particularly good for stimulating the brain, so now might be a good time to take up a musical instrument. Or even conducting! If you think about how long-lived many top musical conductors are – and how vigorous their minds appear to be – there must be something about the combination of grappling with musical notation and feeding your finer senses that keeps people youthful.

Keep learning

Of course, we're not all cut out for musical activities, but large numbers of us are learning other new subjects that appeal to us, in a bid to keep our brains in trim. I mentioned in Chapter 2 how plenty of baby boomers are studying at university to get qualifications to improve their job prospects. But many are studying just for the challenge and the pleasure of exercising their minds and memories.

According to the Higher Education and Statistics Agency, there are 16,220 women in the UK aged between 45 and 65 doing postgraduate or undergraduate degrees full-time, and almost 120,000 doing part-time degrees and postgraduate diplomas. That's a lot of brain boosting!

GET THE HAPPINESS HABIT

When people have good mental health they have a deep sense of happiness and optimism. I said earlier that psychologist Martin Seligman focuses on teaching people to increase their levels of authentic happiness, in a bid to foster good mental health. These days he's not alone. There are various organisations promoting happiness as a proactive route to positive mental health. One of them is the World Happiness Forum, and recently I went to one of their conferences where there was a fascinating mix of delegates and speakers, including politicians, educationalists, philosophers, psychotherapists, psychologists, psychiatrists and religious leaders.

As I listened to them, what struck me was just how much common ground there was between them, despite their disparate backgrounds. And I realised that they were virtually all in agreement on the same ingredients for happiness, which are:

- Altruism
- An enquiring mind
- Healthy eating
- Physical exercise
- Resilience
- A strong social network
- Transcendence

Let's briefly look at them all.

Altruism

This isn't a word we use much, but it's defined in the dictionary as 'unselfish concern for the welfare of others'. Now, you might wonder why altruism should make you happy. You may even think that after years of being at everyone else's beck and call this is your time – and that it would be great if more people could be altruistic towards you! But I want to stress how important it is as we get older that we don't turn in on ourselves and forget that we're part of a larger community. Caring for others is a vital component of happiness. Think for a moment about people you know who are mean-minded and whose mantra is 'Look after Number One'. Are they happy? Are they good to be around? Usually not.

There's now plenty of research to suggest that being altruistic makes us happier and more mentally healthy – because we feel better about ourselves when we reach out to assist other individuals.

Altruism is also recognised as a 'stress-reliever', because it takes us out of ourselves and stops us thinking about our own worries – thereby releasing tension. And altruism can really benefit depressed people, because when they put themselves out for others, this boosts their regard for themselves and helps to stop that damaging sense of being a worthless failure, which is all too common during a depressive illness.

One of the best ways to be altruistic is through being a volunteer of some kind. And you might be interested to read what Professor Felicia Huppert of Cambridge University had to say at the Happiness Conference about volunteering. She claimed that people who live in Scandinavian countries have the greatest sense of happiness and well-being of all Europeans, and that inhabitants of countries from the former Soviet bloc have the least. The rest of us are somewhere in between.

It turns out that 70 per cent of Norwegians are involved in volunteer projects of various kinds, whereas only 7 per cent of Bulgarians are. This doesn't prove beyond doubt that altruism makes you happy, but it's certainly a good argument for the theory.

An enquiring mind

Individuals with ambitions to learn more – whether it's a foreign language or getting to grips with new technology –

stay younger in spirit, and are much more positive, than people who don't.

Healthy eating

Yes, eating healthily helps to make you happy, which is yet another reason to re-think your diet and focus on foods that will do you good and give you energy.

Physical exercise

Well, I hope you're persuaded by now that getting active is crucial if you want to feel well and keep your mind in trim. But exercising also boosts our happiness levels. It gets oxygen pumping around our bodies and brains – making us feel alert and lively – and it also prompts the release of 'happy chemicals', called endorphins, into our bloodstream.

Resilience

We can all become more resilient by identifying the strengths we've developed through the years, and then working out how we can harness them to assist us in solving current or future problems. When we look back over our lives we can all remember difficult times, but we got through them. So, when we feel overwhelmed by some new difficulty, it really helps to remind ourselves that we've got lots of experience in dealing with problems – and to remember what the skills were that we used before. When we do that, we feel more confident about the present problem. And when we're confident, we feel happier.

A strong social network

All the research points to the fact that we are happier people when we have regular contact with friends. As baby boomers, we're very lucky, because most of us have many more mates than our mums ever did – and we have no intention of becoming lonely and friendless. Even being in touch with pals by phone, text or email can boost happiness levels.

Transcendence

This is a rather unfamiliar term, which I'm going to define as 'an exalted state' or as a 'sense of surpassing normal human experience'. In other words, it's a feeling that transports us away from the humdrum and gives us greater perspective. You might get this from organised religion, but more and more of us are finding it in other ways. I don't personally think that it matters whether we achieve transcendence by meditating, or walking by the sea, or meandering around historic buildings, or listening to music, or wandering in the countryside, or looking at great paintings. The important thing is to ensure that we have something in our lives that 'feeds' our souls. When we do, we feel more balanced and happy.

WHERE TO FIND OUT MORE

Authentic Happiness/Positive Psychology:
  www.authentichappiness.com
The World Happiness Forum: www.worldhappinessforum.org

BOOKS

Authentic Happiness: Using the New Positive Psychology to Realise Your Potential for Lasting Fulfilment, by Martin Seligman, published by Nicholas Brealey Publishing

Life Coaching: A Cognitive-Behavioural Approach, by Michael Neenan and Windy Dryden, published by Brunner-Routledge

Mind Over Mood, by Dennis Greenberger and Christine Padesky, published by Guilford Press

Overcoming Depression, by Paul Gilbert, published by Constable Robinson

Spark! How Exercise Will Improve the Performance of Your Brain, by Dr John J. Ratey and Eric Hagerman, published by Quercus

The Science of Happiness: How Our Brains Make Us Happy – and What We Can Do to Get Happier, by Stefan Klein, published by Marlowe and Co.

KEEP HAPPY

Finally, one of the most important parts of the World Happiness Forum conference for me was learning how science demonstrates that we can indeed turn ourselves into happier people. A decade ago, I wrote a book called *Get the Happiness Habit*. One of the things I tried to do in it was encourage people to the view that if they noticed happy things and thought about these things more – instead of dwelling on all the miserable aspects of each day – they could build a habit of happiness. I was doing that kind of work with my clients and I knew it worked. But at the time I wrote the book, I didn't have knowledge of the science that might back up my theories. We have it now!

Because of modern-day scanning and imaging techniques, it's possible to actually look at the activity in people's brains. A researcher at the conference told us that when individuals are being scanned, and they are asked to think about something really pleasurable, there is a sudden burst of activity in the front left-side of the brain, which shows up on the scan.

Physicist and philosopher Stefan Klein says that because of these technological advances, it's now possible to show that the more a person focuses on positive things, the more activity he or she will generate in the part of the brain that registers happiness, well-being and contentment. So it's not a huge leap to believe that any one of us – by thinking more positively and optimistically – can become a happier person. And that's a wonderful notion to hold on to as we grow older.

Of course, I can't guarantee that even if we eat well, exercise regularly and train our brains to be happy we won't ever succumb to depression or dementia – but I hope you'll agree that it's worth trying, in the hope that we'll stay mentally buoyant and alert for decades.

CHAPTER 6

Live Long and Prosper

'Death is a very dull, dreary affair, and my advice to you is to have nothing whatever to do with it.' (W. Somerset Maugham)

There's an awful lot of nonsense talked about how to live longer – and much of it is based on supposition rather than fact. But if we bone up on all the health information that is available to us already – advice that has been scientifically researched and verified – then a great many of us could lengthen our life spans.

Frankly, with all the advantages we baby boomers have had, we ought to live to a ripe old age. However, living longer is only one half of the picture. Do you want to live to be a hundred if you're not fit and happy? I certainly don't. So this chapter is all about what we need to know – and what we can actually do – in order to live long and stay well.

What we fear

You may remember that in Chapter 1 I mentioned how, prior to writing this book, I posted a baby-boomer questionnaire on my website. The results of this survey, which was filled in by a large number of women from the UK and elsewhere, made fascinating reading. I asked what we most feared for the future and:

- 73 per cent of female baby boomers said they dreaded becoming immobile.
- 65 per cent feared losing control of their lives.
- 67 per cent hated the thought of becoming seriously ill in old age.

COMPRESSED MORBIDITY

What we need to aim for is a new concept for ageing called compressed morbidity: the idea being that we live a long and healthy life until we get a final disease or illness, and then pop off very quickly. To put it another way, we would live longer – but die quicker. This sounds tailor-made for our generation. Many of our parents have seemed 'old' for much of their retirement. This is not what we want for us!

But can we achieve compressed morbidity? As I don't have a crystal ball, I can't tell you for sure, but what I am sure about is that we'll have a good chance of achieving it if we do all the things I've focused on in the previous two chapters, such as healthy eating, regular exercise, keeping our weight down and remaining mentally active.

ARE HEALTH CHECKS HELPFUL?

Far more of us than our mothers have private health insurance – either funded by ourselves or our employers. Lots of us also go for private health assessments – which very few of our mums did.

In the UK there is growing provision of free NHS checks. – breast screening is an obvious example. And the Direct Gov website also advises all over-fifties to have regular tests at their family doctors for blood pressure, cholesterol, diabetes, hearing and sight. Many good GP practices routinely call in their female baby boomers for health assessments, but if yours doesn't, you can ask your doc for them.

Checking eye health

Eye examinations are certainly worth having – not just to ensure that you've got the right reading glasses, but because optometrists and ophthalmic opticians can sometimes spot signs in your eyes that indicate illnesses such as high blood pressure or diabetes.

You'll also be checked for glaucoma, which, if left undetected and untreated, would lead to damage in the optic nerve and eventual blindness. Even more importantly, an eye examination can pick up cases of age-related macular degeneration (AMD). This is a complex condition involving the macula, which is the part of the eye that allows us to see fine detail. AMD can advance slowly, but, worryingly, it sometimes progresses very rapidly indeed and leads to a loss of vision. In fact, it can sometimes spring up between eye tests.

Dr Susan Blakeney of the College of Optometrists says that we should see an optometrist right away if we find that straight lines appear to be blurry or wavy, or have gaps in them. She also says that because this fault sometimes happens only in one eye, we may not notice the problem, as a 'good' eye could be doing all the work. So she suggests that all of us check our own vision once a week by closing one eye at a time, and then looking at something with straight lines, such as a Venetian blind.

If you detect a problem when you do this self-test, please see an optometrist urgently.

Looking after your teeth

Getting your teeth checked is also crucial. Obviously, poor teeth are very ageing, but they're unhealthy too. And if we don't see a dentist – and hopefully a hygienist too – we're likely to get significant gum disease, which will lead to teeth falling out, and other health complications.

Dental checks can also reveal changes in the mouth, which might indicate the presence of anaemia, tongue or other oral cancers, and leukaemia. So seeing a dentist could save your life.

Body checks

What about rather more extensive health checks – in particular private full-body X-ray screening? There's quite a vogue for this in the 'chattering classes'. Dr John Giles, Director of Lifescan – one of the companies offering private CT scans – says that 50 per cent of people get no warning before their first heart attack, which may very well kill them. He also says that UK cancer survival rates are among the lowest in Europe – because of late diagnosis – and that early detection by scanning could save countless lives by giving people information about potential illnesses, which they could act upon. But critics of Lifescan and other similar firms say that scans frequently pick up trivialities, which if they're left alone won't amount to anything – but will seriously worry the patient.

Dr Mark Porter of *The Times* had a scan and was told that he had a number of nodules on his lungs. He said that these turned out to be nothing, but it 'scared the living daylights out of me at the time'. Dr Alan Maryon Davis, Professor of Public Health at King's College London, says:

> *CT scans certainly have a place in preventive medicine. But as with any screening test, there are advantages and disadvantages. They can pick up early signs (e.g. colon polyps over 10mm diameter, early lymphomas, calcified coronary arteries), but they do subject the body to quite high doses of radiation, and should not be used too frequently.*

He's also concerned that a few adults develop a kind of 'check-up neurosis' – and also that some people whose scans are clear, take that as a green light to carry on living an unhealthy lifestyle.

Personally, I think that if you have a family history of a disease that might be picked up early by scanning – and you can afford to pay for this assessment – then you might want to consider it. But I also believe that the best option is to start with all the basic – and cheaper – health tests we're already entitled to. They can give us good information that we can act upon to live well – and longer.

CAN YOU AVOID THE INEVITABLE?

There are unfortunately some conditions that we are more prone to as we age, and these include osteoarthritis and osteoporosis.

Osteoarthritis

It's a depressing thought, but most of us will probably get some osteoarthritis as we grow older. But is it inevitable? Well, it is awfully common: consultant orthopaedic surgeon Dai Rees says that eight out of ten over-50s are likely to be affected by it – especially people who:

- Are overweight – as this puts strain on the joints.
- Have put a lot of stress on joints through sport or their occupation.
- Have had a past fracture, which has caused injury to the joint lining.

Most medical experts say that it's virtually impossible to avoid the condition totally. However, they also say that if we're of normal weight and we're active – and if we avoid putting excessive strain on our joints – we can drastically reduce our chances of getting badly affected. They suggest exercise such as Pilates, walking, yoga, cycling and swimming for building up muscle strength and keeping us supple.

Support group Arthritis Care also recommends that we eat a healthy diet comprising plenty of fruit and vegetables, oily fish, white meat and brown rice. They say it's usually good to lose weight too, because when we do –

even by just a few kilos – we can help to take pressure off our joints and keep them healthy.

Another useful preventive measure – and one that can treat arthritis too – is the supplement glucosamine. Sports physios have been recommending this remedy for some years, but gradually many medics have come round to their point of view.

Consultant rheumatologist Badal Pal says that recent research has shown 1,500mg of glucosamine sulphate daily can be effective in relieving arthritis symptoms – particularly of the knee joints.

So you might want to consider taking it – either for prevention or treatment.

Osteoporosis

There is another 'ageing' disease that we women worry about – and that is osteoporosis. Are we inevitably going to get that? Certainly lots of us have seen signs of it in our own mothers.

Well, there's no doubt that most of us lose bone density as we get older and also that after the age of 50, we've got a 50 per cent chance of breaking a bone because of osteoporosis. But some women are at more risk than others. The National Osteoporosis Society identifies them as those who:

- Have a family history of osteoporosis – most particularly if their mothers have ever broken a hip.
- Have low body weight (particularly if caused by an eating disorder).

- Drink excessive amounts of alcohol or smoke heavily.
- Take high doses of corticosteroid tablets – perhaps for asthma or arthritis.
- Are immobile through illness.
- Have a medical condition that affects the absorption of foods, such as Crohn's disease or coeliac disease.

Exercise is key

If we don't have those risk factors, many of us will be able to help ourselves to keep our bone density loss to a minimum by exercising regularly and by eating plenty of calcium. You might remember that I listed many calcium-rich foods in Chapter 4. These are the items you ought to eat if you're trying to prevent osteoporosis.

As for exercise, it needs to be of the kind where you support your own weight. This means that swimming isn't much good. Instead, you should be walking, dancing, skipping, running, jogging or playing tennis or badminton.

If you have any physical problems – such as arthritis – either your GP or the National Osteoporosis Society will give you advice on what type of exercise would be OK for you.

Keeping active and eating healthily are the best ways we know about for keeping osteoporosis at bay.

Drug treatments

If you do get osteoporosis, there is good and bad news that you need to know about. The good news is that drug treatments are improving all the time. The pills that used to be prescribed were often unpalatable and difficult to tolerate, but now there is a range of newer medications – some of which are only given once a year, by means of a drip.

The bad news is that one of the treatments for osteoporosis, called alendronic acid, might be linked to a condition called osteonecrosis of the jaw (ONJ), which could lead to long-term infection – or even destruction – of the jawbone.

A couple of top dentists have told me that they've seen evidence of this condition in patients – although they both also said that it's incredibly rare. However, ONJ is something you need to know about, and something you need to discuss with your doctor, if you're being treated for osteoporosis.

The sun

For decades, we've been told to cover up in the sun. But now there's growing anxiety that maybe we're not getting enough of it on our skin. Sunlight is a major source of vitamin D, which is hugely important to our well-being – not least because it helps us maintain healthy bones.

Obviously, it would be unwise to sit in tropical sun for hours on end, but many doctors and other experts – including medical journalist Oliver Gillie – now believe that in climates such as Britain, we should get some sun on our faces and arms for about 20 minutes at a time, three times a week. You can find out more from The Health Research Forum.

DIABETES – A DEVASTATING DISEASE

One disease that is very definitely not inevitable is diabetes – and yet we're developing it in huge and unprecedented numbers. The International Diabetes Federation claims that each year seven million individuals develop the condition. This is terrifying. And what's worse is that half of the diabetics in the world don't even know they've got it.

Diabetes can lead to other serious conditions, including blindness, heart and kidney problems – and diabetics account for 50 per cent of the number of people who have to have limbs amputated.

So you don't want to get it, if you can avoid it.

You probably know that there are two types of diabetes. One of them, type-1, tends to occur in younger people. But type-2 diabetes is the really common sort, which mainly occurs in people over 40 – and it happens when we're unable to make enough insulin, or when we can't use it effectively.

Beating diabetes

The best ways to avoid diabetes are to exercise regularly, to eat healthily and to avoid getting overweight. If you are overweight you need to be aware of the usual symptoms of diabetes, so that if you spot them you can get help quickly. They include:

- Feeling thirsty frequently
- Peeing a lot
- Blurred vision

If you experience any of those, go to your doctor. He will do a blood or urine test and quickly establish whether or not you have this illness.

There's lots of information on preventing diabetes – or about living with it if you've got it – on the Diabetes UK website. I also think that everyone should read *The Diabetes Revolution* by Dr Charles Clark. This book pulls no punches and aims to get people to control their diabetes the natural way through diet. Clark says: 'Our bodies do not need, and were never designed to cope with, large quantities of refined carbohydrates such as the immense loads of refined sugars and starches in the pre-packaged foods which form the basis of the modern Western diet.'

Chris McLaughlin, who's the health editor at *Saga* magazine, is a diabetic who has adopted the Clark method. She can eat lean meat, fish and shellfish, olive oil, butter, salads, herbs and spices, and vegetables (except parsnips and potatoes). But she is not allowed many of her favourite foods, which include baguettes, wholemeal bread, croissants, potatoes, pasta – and ploughman's lunches.

When she sticks to the diet, she loses weight and her diabetes improves. However, it's hard for her to maintain it, because it means giving up so many of the foods that she craves. Obviously, being a health editor, she knows that letting her diabetes get out of control is a much worse option than having to alter her diet, but she still finds it difficult. Life as a diabetic is tough – so it's far, far better if you can stop yourself from becoming one in the first place.

If all else fails

My final word on the subject is that there is a new and controversial treatment for people with severe diabetes who are extremely obese. This is obesity surgery in the shape of stomach stapling, gastric bypass or stomach-band surgery. It's a risky business, but there are reports that it can cure the condition. An Australian study claimed that when a patient's stomach size is reduced, he or she is five times more likely to be cured of diabetes than similar patients who are being more conventionally treated.

I doubt whether this treatment will ever become routine. But it is new – and you might therefore want to know about it.

How do you know which health stories to believe?

Almost every day there are fresh newspaper claims about wonder drugs that will completely cure serious illnesses. But are these stories true? Often they're not – or the research quoted is years away from becoming a medical reality.

It's difficult to know what to believe. But there's a marvellous section on the NHS Choice website, called 'Behind the Headlines', which gives a balanced and informed view on all those contentious health claims. So, if you want to find out the real truth, you can.

WHAT WE NEED TO KNOW – AND DO – ABOUT CHOLESTEROL

Another condition we really need to know about is high cholesterol – because this can cause heart attacks and strokes. Cholesterol is a fatty chemical in the blood, which comes mainly from saturated fats in our food. There are two types:

1 LDL (low-density lipoprotein), which is the kind likely to make you ill.
2 HDL (high-density lipoprotein), which is a protective type of cholesterol.

In Britain, the Department of Health cholesterol guidelines are that our LDL cholesterol should be less than 3 units. They also say that our total cholesterol reading should be no more than 5. (In America, a different scale is used.)

I mentioned earlier that the Direct Gov website advises us that once we're 50, we should get our cholesterol checked by having a blood test. This really is vital, because we could be walking around feeling fine at the moment, but have a dangerously high cholesterol level. You can often reduce cholesterol by eliminating saturated fats as much as possible and doing more exercise.

Like many people, I come from a family with a history of heart attacks. So I get my cholesterol levels checked twice a year. Some time ago, my level was too high. So, I worked out how I could alter my lifestyle to get that level down. Basically, I substituted olive oil for butter, ate loads of fish and poultry and upped my intake of fruit and vegetables.

And I eliminated as much saturated fat as possible by cutting out cheese, butter, cream, chocolate, mayonnaise, biscuits, cakes and puddings. I also took more exercise.

In four months, my blood levels had dropped to a more acceptable 4.3 units. Now, I can tell you that because I truly love my life, if it's a question of eating chocolate or living longer, that's a no-brainer for me. But I know that not everyone feels the same. Plenty of people would sooner take medication than give up foods they like. And there are people with high cholesterol who can't manage to bring their levels down by diet alone. So, they're almost certainly going to have to take a type of medication called statins.

Statins – a cure for cholesterol?

There have been suggestions by some drug companies that statins do such a good job, we should all be on them even if our cholesterol is normal. And you may be impressed with that argument. But one of the things that being married to a doctor has taught me is that if a drug is strong enough to do what it's supposed to do, then it's bound also to have side-effects. So I prefer to avoid medication if I can.

The important thing is for us all to keep our cholesterol levels down by a method that really works for us. For more information, take a look at all the advice on the British Heart Foundation's website.

HEART DISEASE KILLS WOMEN

It's not a very cheery topic, but we're all going to die of something. And the biggest single killer of women is heart disease. Are you surprised by that? If so, you're not alone. Many baby boomers have told me they thought that breast cancer was our likeliest killer. So, it's vital for us to accept that heart disease – and sudden heart attacks in mid life – aren't just something blokes get. They can happen to us too. But how can we prevent them?

Dr Mike Knapton, the British Heart Foundation's Director of Prevention and Care, told me that there are three major rules to remember:

1 Don't smoke.
2 Get control of your weight.

3 Find a way to exercise – because as you get older, it can seem harder to keep fit.

He said, 'Research shows that even moderate activity will make you much healthier than you would be if you just sat around all the time.' And he also told me about a 2008 study which demonstrated that people who drink moderately, exercise, quit smoking and eat five servings of fruit and vegetables each day, live, on average, 14 years longer than people who adopt none of these behaviours.

So, it's really worth remembering that even if we just make a few improvements in our lifestyles, the health of our tickers is likely to improve.

───────── **BABY-BOOMER FACT** ─────────

New research published in the British Medical Journal in 2009 showed that women with a resting pulse rate of 76 and over are more likely to have a heart attack than women with a lower pulse. Can we bring our pulse rate down? Yes we can – by exercising more.

The symptoms of heart disease

I think it's tough for us to get our head around the idea that heart disease is the illness most likely to carry us off – so I believe we should all be familiar with what the common symptoms of heart disease in women are. They're listed on the British Heart Foundation website, and they include:

- A dull pain, ache or 'heavy' feeling in the chest.

- A mild discomfort in the chest that makes you feel generally unwell.
- Pain in the chest, which may spread to the back, stomach or left arm.
- A chest pain that feels like a bad episode of indigestion.
- Feeling a bit light-headed or dizzy as well as having chest pain.

If you ever get any of these, see a doctor immediately.

The right kind of red wine

According to *The Wine Diet* by Roger Corder, it's not just any red wine that will help your health, but a special kind. Corder claims that the best wines to drink are those rich in procyanidins – such as those made from Tannat grapes and produced in the Madiran region of Gascony – because they actually inhibit the build-up of fatty plaques in the arteries.

CANCER

Although we now know that heart disease is the number-one female killer, I think that many of us fear cancer above everything else. However, there's plenty of evidence today that altering our lifestyle can maximise our chances of avoiding it – just as with heart disease.

You don't need me to tell you that the most important thing anyone can do is to give up smoking. But there is other health information, which you might not know about, that could help us to avoid the Big C.

In February 2009, The World Cancer Research Fund and the American Institute for Cancer Research published a report called 'Food, Nutrition, Physical Activity, and the Prevention of Cancer'. Here are some of their recommendations:

1 Be as lean as possible, within the normal range of bodyweight.
2 Be physically active: this means aiming to do 30 minutes or more of vigorous activity every day – and limiting sedentary activities such as watching TV.
3 Limit foods that promote weight gain – particularly drinks with added sugar and fast foods.
4 Eat at least five portions of fruit and/or non-starchy vegetables every day. Aim to get these in a wide variety of colours, including red, purple, white, orange and yellow. Tomatoes and garlic are particularly desirable.
5 Don't eat more than 500g (1lb 2oz) of red meat in a week – and avoid processed red meat as much as possible.
6 Cut alcohol consumption to one drink a day.
7 Cut down on salt.
8 Aim to meet nutritional needs though diet alone as opposed to taking supplements.

Those suggestions are all about preventing cancer in general, but what are the types of cancer that we should most fear – and how can we avoid getting them?

Breast cancer

This is the UK's most common form of cancer in women – although lung cancer is a bigger killer. One in ten of us reading this book is likely to have, or have had, or will get, this disease. And we've all known women who've had it. Indeed – and very sadly – some of us have lost close and lovely friends or family because of it.

For that reason, it's common sense to take responsibility for knowing our breasts and looking out for any signs that their appearance has altered. So, we should regularly check for lumps, lumpiness, changes in shape, any dimpling in the skin, and the state of our nipples. And if there's discharge, or a nipple becomes in-turned, we should see a doctor right away.

Breast screening

Now I'm sure we all know that we should check our breasts. But do we all do it? No, we don't. However, there's good news in that UK breast-cancer deaths peaked in 1989, and that since then the numbers of women dying of the disease have dropped by 36 per cent. Experts attribute this decrease to the NHS breast-screening programme.

In Britain, those of us aged between 50 and 70 are routinely called for breast screening every three years, and by 2012, the age range will widen to include every female aged 47 to 73. But the programme is not without its critics – and there's growing controversy about treatment post-screening.

Dr Peter Gøtzsche, Director of the Nordic Cochrane Centre at the University of Copenhagen, said in the *British*

Medical Journal that when women are invited for breast screening they're not told of 'the major harm of screening, which is over-diagnosis, and subsequent over-treatment of healthy women'.

Other doctors are worried that women are being put through intense anxiety and invasive treatment when a small abnormality is found, which might not turn into anything nasty if it were left alone. They argue that active monitoring at this early stage might be preferable to surgery.

Finding out about treatment options

So, if a woman attends for screening and is later advised that she has a problem, she should discuss possible treatment options with a specialist.

Of course, it's hard to remember to do this when you're given bad news and you're in a spin of worry, but try to keep calm and to at least ask if there are any other alternatives to surgery. Some specialists, for example, now offer chemotherapy before surgery, which could well shrink the tumour. So, try to have a discussion about treatment. That way you'll feel more in control of the situation.

A possible link to sleep?

Something else you need to know is that recent research studies have linked breast cancer to a lack of, or disrupted, sleep. Research from Japan's Tohoku University Graduate School of Medicine in which a scientific team analysed 24,000 women aged between 40 and 79, found that those women who regularly slept for six hours or less a night were 62 per cent more likely to develop breast cancer than those who slept for seven hours. There have also been reports that shift workers are more prone to breast cancer – because of either sleep deprivation, or possibly through increased exposure to artificial light. In March 2009, the Danish government started paying compensation to some workers who had breast cancer, and who had worked long shift hours. So, if you've done a lot of night work – maybe as a nurse or a flight attendant – you should be extra-vigilant in checking your breasts and never missing a mammogram.

Genetic factors

One last thing: because breast cancer is so common and occurs in one in ten women, it's not surprising if you have at least one relative with it. However, if you have three close blood relatives (from the same side of your family) who developed breast cancer, or any other worrying female cancer history, then you should talk to your GP about being referred to a genetic testing clinic.

Ovarian cancer

Most of us know far less about ovarian than breast cancer. Certainly, we don't tend to learn specific health messages about preventing it, as we do for other cancers. But the support organisation called Ovarian Cancer Action says that we can help ourselves by never ignoring:

- Persistent pelvic and abdominal pain.
- Increased abdominal size and persistent bloating (not bloating that comes and goes).
- Difficulty in eating – and feeling full quickly.

You may also have heard that there could be a link between using talcum powder on the genital area and getting ovarian cancer. But this hasn't been proved. Personally, I've always felt anxious about contracting ovarian cancer, as I know that so often women don't find out that they have it until it's too late to cure it. So, about every 18 months, I go for a pelvic scan, in the hope that it would pick up the beginnings of the disease in time to do something about it.

As far as I know, there are no current plans to make pelvic scans available to all on the NHS, although women at particular risk for genetic reasons should be able to get them. If you have private health insurance, your insurance company might fund pelvic scanning. If not, you'll have to pay if you want it – and charges for the procedure are about £150.

Womb cancer

What you need to know about womb cancer is that it mostly occurs in women of over 40. If you're still having periods, you should see your doctor if your bleeding becomes heavier or irregular, as this could sometimes be the first sign of womb cancer. And if you've stopped menstruating, you need to be aware that any sudden and unexpected vaginal bleeding could indicate possible womb cancer.

Because bleeding is the first symptom – which is an obvious one – and this type of cancer develops slowly, most women who have it get treated before it's very advanced. In such circumstances, cure rates are high. Treatment in 90 per cent of cases is by having a hysterectomy.

No one knows exactly what causes womb cancer – although hormone treatment can provoke it – but over-weight women are twice as likely as other women to get it.

Soya might help

Something else of interest is that Cancer Research UK has reported that some studies show eating phytoestrogens may make women less likely to get womb cancer. You can boost your levels of these substances by eating more soya products.

Cancer of the cervix

The most important thing you need to know about cancer of the cervix is that it's most common in women over 50. So it's vital that you carry on having regular smear tests – and don't assume that only younger women get it.

Smear tests pick up abnormalities before they have a chance to develop into anything more sinister. Symptoms of cervical cancer include post-sex bleeding, bleeding between periods, bleeding after the menopause and a brown discharge. But it's best to catch it before it produces symptoms.

You may know that there is now an anti-cervical cancer jab. Very few baby boomers have had it – but those who have must bear in mind that smears are still essential because the injection can't give total protection.

Lung cancer

It might surprise you that lung cancer kills more of us than breast cancer does, although I don't think it will surprise you that cigarette smoking is still the most likely cause of it. However, if you're a smoker, don't assume that if you stopped now it would be too late to do you any good. When someone stops smoking, the risk of lung cancer begins to fall quite rapidly. And the organisation Cancer-backup says that after 15 years, your risk of getting it would be no greater than that of a non-smoker.

Bowel cancer

The main thing you need to know is that you should never ignore blood on toilet paper after going to the loo. Although this may just indicate that you've got piles, it could be a sign of bowel cancer. You also need to know that bowel cancer may run in families. It's thought that a high-fibre diet helps protect against this common disease.

The good news

Finally, on the subject of cancer as a whole, you might be heartened to know that in the summer of 2009, Cancer UK reported that deaths from the disease were at their lowest since 1971.

STARVE YOURSELF – AND LIVE LONGER?

So far, practically all the recommendations for every illness and condition I've talked about in this book have suggested we should keep our weight within normal limits. But some people believe that if you're determined to extend your allotted time on this earth, you need to weigh much *less* than normal.

The research supporting this theory isn't new. Since 1934, scientists have known that they can double the life of a rat or a mouse by giving it a low-calorie diet. As for people, scientists have long studied the lifestyles of the Okinawan population, who are renowned for their longevity.

For cultural reasons, the Okinawans only ever eat until they are 80 per cent full. Is this why they have such extended lifespans? Some scientists think it is. They also think that what destroys life is the augmentation of free radicals (unstable molecules), and that people like the Okinawans, who eat low-calorie diets, have fewer free radicals in their blood, and therefore do less damage to their DNA.

The secret of longevity?

Obviously, as most people want to live longer, this is a fascinating subject and scientists keep researching it.

In the summer of 2009, for example, a new study, which had been conducted on monkeys over a 20-year period, was published by the University of Wisconsin. Half the animals had been on a severely restricted diet (30 per cent of normal food intake) – and only a fifth of those had died during that time, whereas half the control group had died. The 'starved' monkeys were also healthier with fewer heart problems and cancers, and fewer had diabetes.

Obviously, monkeys are a closer relation to us than mice are, so this research does have relevance for humans. But, commenting on the story for the BBC, Catherine Collins of the British Dietetic Association said, 'People would have to weigh up whether they are prepared to compromise their enjoyment of food for the uncertain promise of a longer life.' She also said that they could be plagued with all sorts of health problems including osteoporosis.

Whatever the theories, an increasing number of people are adopting a stringently low-calorie diet in the hope of living longer. If you want to join them, there's plenty of information on the Internet about calorie reduction (CR) and its claims about longevity. But when you think that 69 per cent of us baby boomers are officially overweight, I'm not sure there'll be too many of us keen to starve ourselves in the hope of having a few more years of life. It would require real discipline and you couldn't even have a scoop of Ben and Jerry's on your birthday!

ANTI-AGEING MEDICINE

Finding ways of extending our lives has become very big business in the medical and pharmaceutical arenas. In 1993, mindful of all the staggering developments in science and technology that will lead to us living longer, 12 physicians in America got together and formed the Anti-Ageing Medicine Movement. Since then, it has mushroomed – and thousands of doctors and scientists worldwide now belong to it. There are some very eminent individuals involved – and some pretty wacky ones too.

When I went to an Anti-Ageing conference in London not long ago, there were an awful lot of people wandering around with weirdly coloured chestnut hair atop pretty worn and old (although sometimes botoxed) faces. And that was just the fellas!

But there is no doubt that there are huge developments in medicine and science happening right now – and that yet again as a generation we're in the right place at the right time.

I think, however, it would be premature to assume we can neglect all the health messages that have formed the backbone of my last three chapters. But, I could be wrong.

Dr Aubrey de Grey, a biomedical gerontologist from Cambridge, believes that once mankind has cracked the difficulties in reaching the age of 150, then carrying on to 1,000 will be a doddle. In fact, he claims it's possible that the person who will first live to be 1,000 may be alive today – and could even currently be in mid life!

New developments in drugs

I think that is stretching belief a bit far myself – but other developments are much more certain; for example, some scientists reckon that by around 2015, about half the drugs available will be designed to meet people's individual genetic profile. At present, if you get a disease such as cancer, your specialist will make a reasoned judgement about which medication to prescribe for you. But he won't know for sure how you'll react to it, and as a result, he may have to adjust the dose, or try you on several different drugs before your condition improves, but all this could change. It's entirely conceivable that before long, your doctor will be able to use blood tests to see which genetic variations you have, and will then have a much clearer idea about which medicine will suit you best. This will cut out a lot of time – as well as trial and error.

It certainly isn't too fantastical or futuristic to suppose that before too much longer, through DNA testing, we will be able to find out which diseases or conditions we're more likely to get – and therefore which particular preventive measures we need to take.

Anti-inflammatory and antioxidant eating

Some nutritionists and gerontologists believe that ageing is largely due to increased inflammation in the body as we age, and that this is the basis of chronic pain and damage to our immune system.

They advocate diets rich in anti-inflammatory foods, which include: olive oil, walnuts, grapeseed oil, cold-water oily fish such as salmon and trout, lean poultry and soya beans.

Many scientists also believe that free radicals cause damage to our DNA and that as we grow older, our bodies are less able to repair it. They say that you can counter this damage by eating foods rich in antioxidants, such as dried apricots, prunes, dates, cherries, blueberries, raspberries, pomegranates, grapes, soya beans, pecan nuts, walnuts, hazelnuts, sunflower seeds and oats.

Spare parts

Another advance will come with the increasing techno-logical capability of harvesting people's own cells in order to cure them of various diseases, or even to produce new body parts – which certainly gives fresh meaning to the phrase 'grow your own'!

This development is already under way in the treatment of some cancers and is beginning to be applied in transplants. So, in the future, if your bladder is diseased, or your knee cartilage is banjaxed, your own cells may come to the rescue and provide you with the relevant new bits.

WHERE TO FIND OUT MORE

American Institute for Cancer Research: www.aicr.org
Arthritis Care: www.arthritiscare.org.uk
Behind The Headlines:
    www.nhs.uk/News/Pages/NewsIndex.aspx
British Heart Foundation (BHF): www.bhf.org.uk
Cancer Research UK: www.cancerresearchuk.org or
    www.cancerhelp.org.uk
The College of Optometrists: www.college-optometrists.org
Diabetes UK: www.diabetes.org.uk
Health Research Forum: www.healthresearchforum.org.uk
International Diabetes Federation: www.idf.org
Lifescan UK: www.lifescanuk.org
National Osteoporosis Society (NOS): www.nos.org.uk
Ovarian Cancer Action: www.ovarian.org.uk
World Cancer Research Fund: www.wcrf-uk.org

BOOKS

The Diabetes Revolution, by Dr Charles Clark and Maureen
    Clark, published by Vermilion
The Wine Diet, by Roger Corder, published by Sphere

CONSTANT PROGRESS

What masses of medical advances we've seen over the years. And if we live long enough, there may yet be some that are beyond our wildest imaginings. It's all a very far cry from the gripe water, Vicks chest rubs, and Minadex tonic of our childhoods. How times have changed!

CHAPTER 7

If You've Got it – Flaunt it!

'If you have big tits, don't wear them round your waist: wear a bra.' (Joanna Lumley)

Unless we looked like the divine Ms Lumley in our youth, we have little hope of resembling her in mid life. But what we can do is to make the very best of what we've got. So, this chapter is aimed at keeping us looking absolutely fabulous!

WE'VE DONE IT OUR WAY!

One of my earliest memories is of being strapped into my pushchair on a cold day and being wheeled to my brother's christening. I can remember exactly what I was wearing — it was a wool coat, with a Fair Isle knitted beret, and matching mittens, which were threaded through the sleeves of the coat on long elastic so that they didn't get lost. I remember feeling happy in that outfit. It seemed like a good look.

That didn't last, of course. Through my later childhood I was aghast at much of what my mother chose for me. The fact is that fashion was undergoing a revolution, and although we dearly loved our mums, we didn't appreciate their taste in clothes.

Nowadays, it's quite gratifying that our daughters and nieces often raid our wardrobes. But we wouldn't have been seen dead in all those safe 'costumes' that our mums had, or with all those accessories — gloves, hats, bags and shoes — that had to match each other.

We thought that our mothers' dated fashion rules were ridiculous. But then, as we started buying our own clothes, our mums thought we looked pretty ridiculous too! I suppose it's fair to say that we had some fashion lows as well as highs, but in most cases we thought we were the cat's whiskers.

MY, WE WERE SO GORGEOUS!

Some of us even got into punk fashion — and if our poor mothers had hated everything that went before that, they were in state of apoplexy over the clunky boots, spiky hairdos and all those safety pins. But hey — we thought we were cool.

As for the 1980s, we were really glam with our huge hair and shoulder pads. Did I hear a whisper that they're coming back? Good-oh!

Fashion highs and lows

What a variety of options we had as we progressed through the 1960s and 1970s:

Mini-skirts

Maxi-skirts

Midi-skirts

Winkle-pickers

Long white boots

Chisel-toed shoes

Platform shoes

Trapeze-line dresses

Kaftans

Cheese-cloth blouses

Afghan-trimmed jackets

Tank tops

Wide-bottomed hipster trousers

Hot pants

Psychedelic prints

Iridescent disco gear

But whatever trends appear, or reappear, there's no way we'll be settling for staid, sober and comfy gear over the next few decades. Why should we? We're far too young for that – and plenty of women of our generation and older are still looking great.

We loved Dame Helen Mirren for her red bikini moment. Twiggy is as iconic as she ever was. And we adore the fact that Britain's oldest model – Daphne Selfe – is still totally stunning despite having been born in 1928!

UNDERPINNINGS

These days what we wear on top may be less important than what we're wearing underneath. It doesn't seem very long since we were being urged to burn our bras. Now, if we've got any sense, we're buying the best we can afford.

If you look carefully at younger women, you'll see that most of them have a greater distance between the fullest part of their breasts and their waist than we do. So, any bra that can help to increase that distance is good news.

Christine Balian, a Frenchwoman who runs a Sussex lingerie business called Desirée, says that when she first came to the UK she was shocked to discover that successful,

---

You're a baby boomer if . . .

- You had a geometric haircut inspired by Vidal Sassoon.
- You ever shopped in Biba.
- You read *Nova* magazine.
- You wore false eyelashes at all times – even down to the local shops!
- You used pan stick as a foundation – in a rather unrealistic tan colour.
- You backcombed your hair.
- You modelled your look on *Charlie's Angels*.

---

well-heeled women often wore grey, sagging bras and limp, off-white knickers under their expensive suits.

Even today, she feels that we don't prioritise our underpinnings like her fellow-countrywomen do. In French towns it's common to find five lingerie shops in a street. Here, there's one about every eight miles!

Maybe we've just never quite cottoned on to the fact that a properly fitted bra makes all the difference to posture, confidence and silhouette. Christine says that most women in the UK think they know their size, but are usually wrong. So, when we buy a bra from a department store without trying it on, or having it properly fitted, we often select one that's too tight, which means that our flesh balloons out in awkward places. Getting the right brassiere makes all the difference.

A good bra for confidence

Recently, a politician with an ample figure came to Christine's shop for the first time — and went away with a beautiful, perfectly fitting bra. The next day she came back and said that her new brassiere had made her feel so confident, she wanted four more!

So, what we're putting under our clothes is important if we're trying to feel great about ourselves and make the best of what we've got.

Quick tip

Improve your posture by imagining that your head is suspended by elastic from above. Lengthen your neck and keep your shoulders down, and pull up from the waist so that you lift up your whole rib cage.

People learn this kind of stance in yoga or ballet, but you can do it for yourself. And it will genuinely help you feel younger, slimmer and more confident.

INVISIBLE? I DON'T THINK SO!

The heartfelt cry from some women of our age is that once past 50 you become invisible. I don't go along with this at all. OK, it's true that young men no longer tend to whistle at us in the street. But that's only because they're programmed by nature to be attracted to women they can impregnate with their sperm, and thus continue their tribe. Whether we like it or not, we no longer qualify. And you can't overcome millennia of conditioning just like that! But if we are invisible, it's because we're not properly expressing our real selves. We don't have to be beautiful to achieve that. We just need to do our own thing.

The other day I happened to see two women of around 55 who looked knock-'em-dead-gorgeous, but neither was conventionally good-looking. The first had bright scarlet hair. It was very short and gelled and spiky, and it looked great – especially as she had teamed it with matching, dramatic red and black spectacles and a colourful outfit. She was demonstrating a new brand of olive oil in John Lewis's food hall – and she was a real showstopper.

The other woman I noticed also had short hair – black in her case – which she had swept straight back from her forehead. Again, lots of gel was involved. Her make-up was dramatic – lots of bright fuchsia lipstick and matching eyeshadow – and she was wearing a wondrous asymmetric coat. Now, I know this look wouldn't be everyone's cup of tea, but she sure as hell didn't go unnoticed. She looked marvellous.

My point is that we're far too young to opt for broad shoes and elasticated waistbands, sensible skirts and boring blouses.

How to dress now

Of course, this is a transitional time for us, and it can be hard to know how to dress if, for example, you're giving up a City job and planning to work from home, or look after your grandchild, or do some voluntary work. You might always have seen yourself as a tailored sort of person, and have a wardrobe full of dark suits, but now feel unsure what to wear. Maybe you don't have anything in between business clothes and sports gear.

So, who are you now — and how do you want to look? You could be classic, smart casual, hippy, elegant, wacky, preppy, colourful, or flouncy — or all of these things on different days.

Cast your mind back to when you felt at your best. What fashions were you wearing? What colours? We made some fashion faux pas in the past — but that's how we learned about our own style. We might still make mistakes while we work out how we want to look now. But let's not be boringly invisible.

Of course you may be worried that as you get older, you're going to have less money to splash around, but you'll probably have more time. So, you'll be able to shop at leisure in all sorts of places, and get bargains and put together clothes and accessories to reflect the person you've become.

Use some diversionary tactics

Don't forget, we started life feeling timid, and we grew quite bold. Let's stay that way. And if your body has bits you hate, experiment with drawing attention away from them by accessorising with clunky jewellery, or vibrantly coloured scarves, or by wearing seriously sexy shoes. Mostly our feet don't get fat! You can wear black all over to slim you down and then express your exuberance with bright red or leopard-skin shoes.

I hope I don't die before finally finding the perfect pair of black trousers

Have you ever found them? I'm always sure that the pair I'm trying on in the shop are absolutely the ones, only to find after wearing them a couple of times that they're not. Still, I believe we should all have plenty of ambitions to keep us young – and the quest for the perfect black trousers should keep us stimulated for decades.

HIGH HEELS R US!

Talking of shoes, we learned early on how to stride out in stiletto heels – even if our dads did protest about the damage we were inflicting on the floors in the house. High heels make legs look great and they give us a lift emotionally as well as literally.

In 2009, the department store Debenhams conducted a shoe survey, which found that the average woman wears high heels for 51 years of her life. A spokesperson for the company said, 'When women finally abandon high heels, it's an all too public admission that they are getting older. Naturally many women want to postpone this evil day for as long as possible.'

Personally, I think we should carry on exercising our expertise in high heels until we drop – even if we have to walk to a function or a party in trainers, and change into our sensational shoes when we get there.

HEMLINES

What about skirt lengths? After all, we've experimented with every conceivable hemline in our time. But if we always favoured short skirts, can we still carry them off? Definitely! If your legs are great, why shouldn't you show them? You could say that this is what opaque tights were designed for: we can wear shortish skirts but not offend the populace with the less-than-perfect state of our knees.

The great thing about fashion now is that anything goes. Some women look marvellous in floor-length flowing skirts. Others look gracious and elegant with a mid-calf hemline. Lots of us can get away with on-the-knee, which always looks so much more flattering than a hemline ending just below, and a few — a lucky few — can get away with shorter than that.

I was amused to read that the fantastically gorgeous Jerry Hall has been told by her equally beautiful daughter that she's too old for mini-skirts. I suppose that's one of the things that daughters are for!

NO-GO AREAS

However, unless you're prepared to put in almost the same number of hours per week in the gym as Madonna, it makes sense to keep your upper arms covered — except on the beach. Also, there is a golden rule that once past 45, you can bare your cleavage, or your legs, but never both together. That 'Wives and Girlfriends' look beloved of professional footballers' partners often doesn't even suit young women – but it's absolutely hideous on us.

CLOTHES FOR THE WOMEN WE ARE NOW

In a recent article in the Style section of the *Sunday Times*, various famous mothers and daughters talked about how they swap clothes. This is apparently called trans-generational dressing. The European brand Comptoir des Cotonniers has identified this as such a trend that they run casting sessions for mothers and daughters every year – and use the winners as models for their website.

Even if we don't have daughters, these days most of us shop in the same places as people who are 30 years younger than us. High Street favourites such as Top Shop or Zara are packed with women of a certain age picking up state-ment-jackets or fabulous footwear. And charity shops – which have become 'in' places since we've adopted thriftier habits in the recession – appeal across all age ranges.

Nowadays, none of us needs to shop in one place for a whole outfit in the same colour and with matching acces-sories. Instead, we can be eclectic – just like our young relatives and friends – and pick up trousers in one place, a top in another and an accessory somewhere else. Fashion really is fun, if you let yourself go for it.

Designer items at knock-down prices

Don't forget outlet shopping. My friends laugh at me because I'm a TK Maxx shopper. They simply can't understand why

I would plough through rails and rails of unsuitable stuff in the hope of finding a hidden gem. But I love it! In fact, wherever I go, I check if there's a branch there. So far, I've shopped in Cardiff, Newcastle, Hatfield, Croydon, Harrow, Hammersmith (that's a great one), High Street Kensington and in my nearest shop in Brighton.

Through the years, I've had fantastic items by great designers including Betty Jackson, Jasper Conran, Paul Costello and Ronit Zilkha.

Shopping in comfort

I do know that many baby boomers find clothes-shopping a bit of a chore — all that stripping off and finding you look awful in something, and getting all hot and bothered and having to get dressed again to go back on to the shop floor to find something else that might be better. Exhausting!

But there's a solution to that problem — and it's online shopping. Now that all the high-street favourites — including Marks & Spencer, Debenhams, House of Fraser and Next — provide this service, we can purchase and try on clothes in peace and quiet at home.

And there's catalogue shopping too.

Do you remember . . .

. . . those first catalogues? I remember the pretty awful efforts that were around when we were teenagers. I recall paying something like 2s 6d a week over 20 weeks for a dress, which looked great until it was washed — when it went flabby and awful. That felt like an expensive mistake at the time.

Catalogue shopping these days is totally different. A friend of mine buys wonderful clothes from Elégance. They're not cheap – but they're beautifully made. Then there's Kaleidoscope – who create fashion for all shapes and sizes – and Boden, who are great at smart casuals. But there are lots more, and you can find them all through a website called UK Shopping Catalogues.

Common-sense tips

Over the years I've picked up a few tips here and there:

1 Wear a bit of white or cream near the face – it lights it up.
2 There's no point slathering on expensive face creams if you're putting them on top of dead cells. Scrupulous cleansing and regular exfoliating is crucial.
3 Sleep is the greatest beauty secret. Eight hours a night is rejuvenating.
4 Whatever creams and potions you're using on your face, put them on your neck too.
5 A touch of blusher under the less-than-perfect bits of the jawline makes it look more defined than it really is.
6 A hint of white or cream eyeshadow just under the highest point of the eyebrow opens up the space between the eyebrow and the eye. This is an area that tends to collapse as we grow older, so anything that opens it up will help make us look younger.
7 Our jewellery often looks dated – especially if we wear matching earrings, bracelets and necklaces as

we did in years gone by. But worse than that, if we're carrying too much weight, we need to avoid dainty stuff. It emphasizes our bulk rather than detracting from it. Try a big bold necklace or bracelet instead.

8 Take your daughter, niece or male gay friend shopping with you. Allow them to pick out items you'd never have considered. You may not like what they choose, but trying on different outfits might help you broaden your outlook — and you may be surprised by what you look good in.

9 We wear 20 per cent of our wardrobe 80 per cent of the time. So have a clear out. You might find items that you've forgotten. Maybe you can customise them and press them into service.

10 If you need reading glasses, always put them on to check your make-up before leaving the house. It's a bit of a shock to find flecks of eyeshadow on your cheeks, or that your mascara looks clumpy, or that you've overdone the blusher — but far better that you discover this yourself than go out like that.

GET YOUR COLOURS RIGHT

In the 1980s, I presented a TV programme where we 'made-over' six viewers. One of the experts on that programme was a woman who specialised in 'doing' people's colours. There was quite a vogue for that back then. I think it would be a good idea now to check what colours we look best in — because even if we had them done all those years ago, we might suit different colours now. After all some of our own natural colouring has altered!

You don't have to consult an expert – although of course you can. All you need is to get lots of different scarves or colour swatches and hold them one at a time under your chin while you look in the mirror. You will immediately see that some shades flatter and others don't. Some in fact light up your face, whereas others drain it of colour.

Learning whether you are a blue/grey/bluey-pink/ lavender sort of person, or one who looks better in gold and russet colours, will save you huge amounts of money. That's not to say that you can't ever break out and buy something different, but if you mostly stick to the colour range you've selected as flattering, you'll tend to shop for those colours – and most things in your wardrobe will then go with everything else.

HELMET HEADS

Let's now turn our attention to hair, because if we don't get that right, we ruin everything. I've noticed that a lot of female baby boomers wear snazzy outfits but that they're completely let down by short, nondescript, easy-to-care-for, unfeminine hairdos. No wonder young men often refer to women of our age as 'helmet heads'. Not very flattering is it?

The thing is that unless we have the gamine good looks of the late Audrey Hepburn, these no-nonsense haircuts rarely do us any favours.

I know someone who runs an exclusive dating service.

And she often encourages her older female clients to grow their hair a bit and to wear it in a softer style. She knows that these women aren't doing themselves justice – and that unless they do so, it won't be easy to help them find a new partner.

AND DON'T FORGET YOUR TEETH

If you're American, or Canadian, or Swedish, or Danish, you've probably got perfect teeth. Unfortunately, the same can't be said of us in the UK. In fact a Scandinavian dentist said to me that many British people would sooner pay veterinary bills than dental fees!

But bad teeth are very ageing as well as unhealthy. Of course if our teeth fall out, the NHS will come to the rescue and give us false ones, but I think that most of us would want to avoid that. There are all sorts of techniques for improving our own teeth these days. So, if you hate yours – particularly if you don't smile because of them – then visit a dentist and find out what sort of money you'd need to spend to turn them into a thing of beauty.

Teeth whitening is one option. Crowns, bridges and implants are possibilities too, if you have the money. Another one is partial dentures.

Charlotte Stilwell, who's a specialist in prosthodontic dentistry, tells me that one in six adults in the UK has a partial denture. She says: 'The modern partial denture is carefully designed to work with – and protect – the remaining natural teeth and gums. The denture should feel secure and blend in to create a natural smile.'

Unfortunately, if you go to the sort of dentist who's experienced in this work, it won't come cheap, but you may decide that it's a good investment, and that even if you have to forego a holiday, or re-decorating your house, it'll be worth it to be able to smile with confidence.

Smile - you're on camera

I bet when you were about 25 you winced and groaned when you looked at photos of yourself. But I also bet that when you look at them now you think you were gorgeous! So when you get your next holiday snaps, why not try to enjoy them? Because when you're 85, you'll be looking at these and thinking how great you looked. Wouldn't it be nice to believe that now?

STRESS IS VERY AGEING

Smiling is very important if we want to look youthful – and relaxed. Frankly, if you look stressed, you can have the greatest hairstyle in the world, the best teeth and most fabulous frock and you'll still look older than you are.

The other day, I was trying to get a train to London for an important meeting when there was a points failure – and all trains were cancelled. I was really stressed. Suddenly, as I paced the station concourse in Brighton, I caught sight of my fraught face in a shop window. Not a pretty sight. I looked 20 years older than when I had left home that morning.

We often let things get to us: things that are not a matter of life and death. But this doesn't do us any favours. Scientists at an Anti-Ageing conference in London reported that people who've been under a lot of stress for 18 months or more look ten years older than the average person of the same age. So, get de-stressing now – whatever it takes! After all, various experts have calculated that only about 8 per cent of our worries are actually worth bothering about. So, save your stress hormones for those occasions – and give your body and face a break.

WHERE TO FIND OUT MORE

Boden: www.boden.co.uk
Comptoir des Cotonniers: www.comptoirdescotonniers.com
Desirée: tel. 01273 586 178
Elégance: www.elegance.co.uk; tel. 0870 990 9904
Kaleidoscope: www.kaleidoscope.co.uk; tel. 0844 556 4100
UK Shopping Catalogues: www.ukshoppingcatalogues.co.uk

FINALLY – LET'S NOT DO THIS . . .

Have you ever caught yourself grunting or sighing when you bend down?

Haven't we all! But if we really want to make the most of ourselves we need to stop this very bad habit. It's one of those things that will make people think we're old – and as you know, we're far too young for that.

Also, we must avoid getting into the habit of doing things

in our own homes that we wouldn't want to do in public. When I was a young teacher, an older schoolmistress, who was nearing retirement, used to lift up her skirt and start pulling down her knickers in the staff room when she was on the way to the loo. How embarrassing is that?

CHAPTER 8

Because We're Worth it!

'I wish I had a twin, so I could know what I'd look like without plastic surgery.' (Joan Rivers)

This chapter is all about beauty – which these days is a big and complex business. Do you remember when your mum was your age? What was her beauty routine? Soap and water? A bit of Pond's cold cream? A hairspray perhaps, and a favourite shampoo? A pale pink nail varnish? Maybe she gave her hair a colour rinse every two months? If she was anything like my mother, all her products fitted on to one bathroom shelf.

We cannot say the same! I estimate that we use six different items for every one our mother had – and our bathroom cupboards are groaning under the weight of them. I sometimes think I'll need to move house just to accommodate all the paraphernalia I buy in my attempt to hold back the clock.

WHAT DO WE WANT?

What we'd like is to look 25 – but to be as happy and confident as we are now. That would be ideal. But we're not stupid. We know we can't knock more than 20 years off our age. So, we'll have to settle for looking as good as we possibly can.

I remember filming an interview with the late Anita Roddick in 1993. She had a great attitude to her own appearance – and she insisted that the cameraman came in really tight on his close-ups. She said to him, 'This is what a woman of 50 looks like. Why be embarrassed about it?'

Did she seem like 50? I couldn't have put an age to her. But what I was bowled over by was that she looked fit, healthy, happy, vital and vibrant – and that the combination of all those things made her truly beautiful. It's a huge pity that we'll never know what she might have looked like at 90.

Can we cream off the years?

What can we realistically expect from anti-ageing skincare? I knew that I was knocking on a bit when I started to be seduced by skin creams that cost more than I'd normally spend on a frock!

Of course, assistants on beauty counters can be incredibly persuasive – but not always helpful. Personally, I'm not impressed to be told by some dewy-skinned 30-year-old that she uses the wonder cream she wants me to buy. Why would I be? She looks great anyway. What I'd like to see is someone using the cream who's 70 – but looks 45!

We all know that potions can't do the same for us as a facelift, but we still live in hope that the next product we buy – in its perfectly shaped and presented jar – will contain a total miracle. And the presentation has a lot to do with our perception of the product.

Beautiful boxes

In 2008, *Psychologies* magazine tested 100 face creams – ranging from luxury buys to budget-priced items – on a group of their readers. The creams were distributed in nondescript packaging, so that the testers had no idea of the make of the product they were to use.

Interestingly, this created some anxiety. One woman said: 'I didn't realise what a brand snob I was. Not knowing the name of the manufacturer made me feel suspicious and slightly vulnerable.' Another said the test made her realise that normally part of the purchasing experience was the 'treat factor' of enjoying and unwrapping the packaging. And a third woman said that being given an unnamed product in a simple container created a different kind of focus on the cream itself.

The products that were most popular in the *Psychologies* test included some from Boots, Avon and M&S. So, probably we don't need to take out a mortgage to fund our anti-ageing skincare. And next time you are tempted to part with a small fortune, maybe you should ask yourself, 'If this weren't packaged so beautifully, would I rate it as highly as I do?'

Skin deep

What we really need to take on board is this: our skin has a very important function, which is to provide a barrier against bacteria and pollutants – and it does this very well. But because of that, despite what some companies may claim, no beauty product can possibly penetrate and nourish the hidden deep-down layers of the skin. However, the race is on to find ways of bypassing the skin's natural 'barrier' function, but we're talking serious science here – and looking at huge safety implications.

It seems likely that it will one day be possible to hide cosmetic ingredients in liposomes – which are tiny structures made of the same material as a cell membrane. If that happens, the skin will be hoodwinked into letting anti-ageing products past its natural barrier. But for now, we need to accept that our favourite potions moisturise and soften the top layer of our skin – and sometimes speed up how quickly new skin cells are formed – but that's all they can do. They cannot take decades off us.

Softening the wrinkles

There is evidence though that anti-wrinkle creams – as opposed to anti-ageing products in general – can soften wrinkles. A Boots product – No7 Protect and Perfect Intense Beauty Serum – has been rigorously tested by scientists at Manchester University who have found that around a fifth of people who used it for six months saw significant improvement in their facial lines.

Hidden ingredients

Did you know that most anti-wrinkle creams contain ingredients that are related to a medication called Retin-A? Retin-A was originally developed as a treatment for acne. But patients who were using it started to notice that it made their skin look younger. You can actually get hold of Retin-A, but you need to ask your doctor if he will write you a private prescription for it, which you would then take to your pharmacist.

It's much stronger than anything you can buy at a beauty counter, so you'll need to use it sparingly. But that means a tube – which usually costs about £15 – will last for ages.

Firming up

Of course, it isn't just wrinkles that we worry about – it's how our skin sags around the jaw area. There are lots of face-firmer serums on the market that claim to give us uplift, and I confess I've tried most of them! My favourites are those made by Roc and Clarins.

As soon as you put the serum on, you get a reassuringly tightening-up feeling and your face looks a little firmer. But it is temporary – probably the effect lasts for a couple of hours at most. Still, on those days where your confidence needs a bit of a boost and you want to look your best, these products are worth a try.

IS INTERNAL SKINCARE A BETTER BET?

Since no amount of skin cream is really able to knock the years off us, what about nourishing the skin from within? Is that more dependable?

There's no doubt that if you eat and drink healthily, then your skin will benefit – as it's the largest organ in the body, so it absorbs a lot of your nutrients. And women who eat nutritious foods and drink plenty of water often have glowing skin that looks younger than it is.

But there's also lots of interest now in increasing elasticity and youthfulness by taking supplements to promote the growth of collagen. You can get collagen capsules from health-food shops, and also from Web companies such as Clear Skin UK. However, the UK market leader in internal skincare is Imedeen, which is sold in the form of tablets made out of protein extracts from deep-sea fish. It has a legion of followers and I'm one of them.

It makes sense to me that something you take internally is more likely to improve your skin than something you plonk on to its outside. A make-up artist at Thames Television recommended Imedeen to me about 15 years ago, and I've been using it ever since.

The Imedeen people have an ultrasound gadget that measures the collagen levels in your skin. So, if you get a scan prior to taking it, and again some time afterwards, you'll get some idea of whether or not your skin is now generating more collagen and becoming younger looking. Hopefully, you'll also be able to notice the difference in the mirror.

Skin brushing

When I first heard about skin brushing in the 1980s I thought it was totally crazy, but recently I've changed my mind. We have loads of skin cells flaking off us every day – although I can never quite establish whether it's millions or billions. Anyway, it's a lot. And it does make sense that body-butters or lotions will be more effective if they don't have to fight through a layer of dead cells first.

Skin brushing takes only a couple of minutes before you jump into the shower or bath. I've been told it's best to brush towards the heart. And obviously it helps if you pick a brush with a long enough handle to reach all of you, and one that is soft and not scratchy – you don't want to end up looking like your cat has attacked you all over!

FACIAL WORKOUTS

Another way you might notice a difference is through facial exercise. It does seem common sense that if we need to exercise our bodies to keep them in shape, then our faces might benefit from 'working out' too. You've probably heard of Eva Fraser and her facial exercises. Maybe you've seen her demonstrating them on TV, or bought her book. She believes that when our skins appear to sag with age, the main problem is that our muscles are collapsing beneath it. This seems entirely reasonable to me, so I booked a session with her.

Eva is gorgeous! She is 80 but could easily pass for 55! I suspect that her youthful appearance isn't totally down to her facial exercises. When I visited her, she was exposing a hint of cleavage, which was utterly smooth and crinkle-free. So, I bet she's taken enormous care of her skin, and that she's also inherited some great genes.

I'd previously tried doing her exercises on my own by using her book, but working with her was totally different. The muscles in my face really ached afterwards, but it was a good feeling.

Has it worked?

It's now five months since that session, and I've been doing the exercises most days. So, what do I look like? Well, my complexion looks healthier – and I think that's because getting your muscles working must increase circulation to the face. Also, I notice that there's been quite a lift around my eyebrows. Now, I hadn't expected – or even hoped – for that. Frankly, all I was concerned about was firming up my jaw line. But I can now see that if the upper part of the face is strengthened, then the whole of it, including the chin and jaw, gets the benefit.

I do notice a real difference. So I am delighted, and will carry on gurning before my mirror. In fact, I'm going back to Eva to learn some more advanced techniques.

I've also interviewed another facial exercises guru called Marja Putkisto. I haven't tried her exercises myself – there are only so many hours in a day – but having seen her DVD I'm sure they would be effective. She claims that doing them not only has a lifting effect on the face but that they're also good for sinus and headache problems as well.

Marja also has exercise programmes for the whole body, which include learning about breathing and visualisation. She's a fascinating woman – and it's no surprise to me that she has a great following, spread over many countries.

21ST-CENTURY MAKE-UP

If you wear make-up, you've probably noticed that many of today's products are extraordinarily light on the skin compared with stuff we piled on in the past. This is particularly true of foundation, which is usually called 'a base' these days. That's good news, because all the expert advice to us boomers is that 'less is more'.

Gunky make-up clogs up the skin and tends to settle in grooves and creases where we'd sooner it didn't. In fact, what works best is if we use highlighters and concealers to hide blemishes or uneven tone, and then just pat on a bit of foundation where it's really needed.

Ariane Poole, who was the beauty presenter on ITV's *This Morning* for five years, says that it's important to keep up with various developments in make-up, rather than conservatively sticking with the same shades and brands that we've always used – because our hair and skin colours are changing.

New tricks

Isn't it great that we never stop learning? I have short nails that are prone to splitting as a result of spending far too many hours at a computer keyboard. So I was amazed to read one day that short nails look far better if they're painted in bold colours. I'd always assumed that a nude varnish would make them look longer.

In trepidation, I painted my unlovely nails a glossy pillar-box red. They looked infinitely better and my hands appeared younger and nicer too. This is a result!

My other mid-life revelation is how marvellous your eyelashes look when they're dyed. A make-up artist told me this, so I promised to give it a go. The dye goes right to the roots of the lashes where the average mascara wand doesn't reach, so it gives great definition to the eyes. I wish I'd done this years ago. Still, better late than never . . .

Personally, I think the most important thing we can do to look younger is to ensure that our base matches our hands. There's nothing more ageing than foundation that's too dark or too tanned – especially if it doesn't quite go into the hairline. Absolutely hideous!

Liz Thomas's make-up tips for the baby boomer

I sometimes appear on Channel 5's *The Wright Stuff*, where my face is usually titivated by Liz Thomas, an independent make-up artist. Here's her advice for us baby boomers.

- **Don't use hard lines on your eyes**. Instead, use a soft eyeliner with a smudger, or eyeshadow to create a softer look. Keep the liner to the outer corners of your eyes. If you put a line right round them, they'll look smaller and more closed up.

- **Avoid matt brown lipsticks**. Instead, opt for sheer lipsticks or lip glosses with pinker tones. Use a clear liner around your lipline first; these are designed to stop your lipstick bleeding.

- **Don't use heavy powdery foundation**. You want to keep your skin looking as fresh as possible, so use a tinted moisturiser or a light foundation containing an illuminator. Avoid looking too matt, so only apply a light translucent powder to your T-zone (centre of forehead, nose and middle of chin) to stop shine.

- **Don't use a pencil to fill in your eyebrows**. Instead, use an eyebrow powder and a fine-tipped brush. Buy a powder in a shade lighter than you think you need and build up the colour gradually. At all costs, avoid harsh lines.

- **Don't apply a stripe of brown blusher to your cheek bones**. Instead, use a peach or pink blusher and apply it to the apples of your cheeks. This will give you a more youthful look.

SHOULD WE WORRY ABOUT WHAT'S IN IT?

'If you wouldn't dream of eating something, think twice before putting it on your skin.' I don't know who first said that – because several experts claim it was them – but whoever it was definitely had a point. Many of us have become interested – and anxious – about what we're eating, so it seems like common sense to concern ourselves with what we might absorb through our skins from cosmetics. Although we know that the skin is a barrier, it might be possible for at least some of what is put on it to seep into the bloodstream – particularly if you have a cut or graze.

Parabens

Particularly worrying are parabens. These are chemicals that are widely used as preservatives in the cosmetics industry. Until recently, they were regarded as totally safe, but there have been several studies, including one in 2004 conducted by the University of Reading, which have found higher than normal levels of parabens in breast cancer tumours. There's no firm evidence yet to say that parabens *cause* breast cancer, but I do think we need to take notice of this research, because once you start checking, you'll find that a hell of a lot of beauty items have parabens in them.

Phthalates

Another concern are phthalates, which are chemicals found in plastics and packaging. They've also been widely used in cosmetics. They are now banned in personal products in Europe – but not worldwide.

There is evidence that they can harm the liver, kidneys and reproductive organs in some animals – and there is anxiety that they could therefore cause damage to humans. Scientists haven't as yet reached agreement on that. However, you might want to check whether these substances are in your beauty products.

Organic ingredients

Many of us think we're buying safely, if the word 'organic' appears on the label. But the Soil Association tells me that although organic food must meet certain legal standards, this rule doesn't apply to beauty products. As a result, masses of companies claim that their beauty products are 'organic' when actually they only contain a minute amount of something like organic lavender oil, and are packed full of the nasties we're trying to avoid.

But now there is a set of Soil Association Health and Beauty Standards, and if you see the Soil Association logo on anyone's literature, shop or website, you can buy their products with confidence.

If you want to know more, do investigate the health-and-beauty part of the Soil Association website – particularly a link from that section to a page titled 'What's Not in a Certified Organic Beauty Product'. This is quite an eye-opener! The 'banned' substances listed on that page include parabens, various detergents, and petroleum jelly.

─────────── **BABY-BOOMER FACT** ───────────

Interestingly, despite the economic downturn, 2008 saw a massive increase of 69 per cent in the purchase of organic health-and-beauty goods in Britain.

Going natural

With the purchase of organic beauty items increasing, it seems we're waking up to how our routine products may not be as healthy as we'd like.

If you want to read a whole book devoted to the subject of organic skincare and cosmetics, I recommend *Naturally Gorgeous* by Charlotte Vøhtz.

I have to admit that I've always thought there's a lot of nonsense talked about herbal and organic products – and if you read the blurb of some companies making 'natural' products, you could be forgiven for believing that everything that grows is good, and anything man-made is bad. This is totally barmy. Plenty of plants are better avoided; for example, you could die by eating rhubarb leaves, deadly nightshade and various types of mushrooms! However, I have to confess that writing this chapter has changed me and that I am now hooked on reading lists of ingredients, even though they're usually so small I have to do this with the combination of my reading specs and a magnifying glass! Furthermore, I am now only using products that don't contain parabens, phthalates and petroleum derivatives.

Is it my imagination, or does my skin breathe more easily? Does it look better? I really think it does.

Age spots

An 'age spot' to one person is merely a freckle to another! But whatever you want to call them, we are more prone to darkish patches – particularly on our hands – as we get older. And they do rather give our age away.

Creams with vitamin C are supposed to help. Retin-A is also a possible treatment. But probably the best thing you can do is to try to stop any more age spots appearing by putting a high-factor sunscreen on your hands – or anywhere else they crop up – every day.

HAIR THINNING

It's a bit ironic that we get more unwanted hair on our faces just at the point when the hair on our head may not be the crowning glory it once was. If your hair is thinning, you might want to consider using a medication called minoxidil, which, in the UK, is sold under the name of Regaine. (It's called Rogaine in some other parts of the world, including the US.)

The drug was originally developed to reduce high blood pressure, but some bald men who were using it found that their hair started to re-grow – so it became a hair-restoring product.

Regaine doesn't help everyone – probably only about a quarter of users. And even if it does work for you, you'll have to keep applying it, because once you stop your hair will thin again. You can buy it over the counter and it costs about £20 for a month's supply. It's certainly worth trying.

HAIR REMOVAL

But what about all the hair that we don't want? In recent years I've been very grateful that we're the age we are, and not 25 years younger. We got into depilation slowly. Dad's razor came in handy – even though we had to hide when he discovered we'd been using it yet again!

The next stage usually was to try depilatory creams (contemporary brands include Veet or Nair) – and loads of us have stayed with them, or with shaving. As a generation we've never been massively into waxing. How different things are for our daughters and nieces – who are slaves to it. Mind you, they have to be. Young men demand it!

The rise of Internet porn has a lot to answer for – and the fashion for waxing is just one of them. Unfortunately, the vast majority of guys under 30 have got most of their sex education from the cyber world, and as a result many of them think that women were born with a Brazilian wax – or never grow pubic hair at all!

Thank heavens that our partners are more tolerant of a bit of fuzz here and there – unless you've gone in for a very young lover of course!

Laser treatments

There is a relatively new way in which we can get unwanted hair removed almost permanently – by lasering it. This has particular attraction for women who are worried about excess facial hair – especially if their trusty tweezers don't seem to keep it at bay. But obviously, you can also get your bikini line, armpits, legs or anything else done too.

You'll probably need six sessions to become totally smooth. But if you're lucky, you may never need to be treated again – although some people do require a treatment top-up again in a few years.

Laser removal is much less painful than waxing. And it may even be cheaper in the long run.

One of the big players in the laser-removal business is the Harley Medical Group, which has branches throughout the UK. Six sessions with them would set you back about £500. It's important that if you're considering this treatment, you start by having a consultation to check whether it would be suitable for you.

In reputable companies, both the initial assessment and the hair removal are carried out by qualified nurses. Don't even consider having it done if this isn't the case.

Cellulite

Have you ever found a cellulite product that really worked? If so, you're very lucky. I notice that athletes like Paula Radcliffe don't have any cellulite at all, and ballet dancers don't either – so I think that rigorous exercise is the only really effective way to keep it at bay.

Recently, though, there have been claims that you can sculpt your bottom, improve your posture, help any back problems you may have – and drastically reduce your cellulite – by wearing shoes that exercise and activate muscles you may not be using.

MBT shoes are one of the market leaders, Fit Flops are another.

Maybe they're worth a try . . .

MORE THAN MAKE-UP

Let's now look at some of the other treatments available that offer more than make-up ever can, but which stop short of surgery.

Facials

Loads of women swear by facials; others can't fathom why anyone would bother with them. I've always been in the latter camp, but lots of baby boomers are into the modern type of facials – those regarded as 'non-surgical facelifts' rather than those that just unblock your pores. And some women swear by them and regard them as a real rejuvenating treat. A friend of mine said: 'My jowls would be drooping on to my chest if I didn't have one of these treatments every few weeks.'

The main types of 'facelifting' facials are:

- LIA (lymph drainage, incandescent massage and acupressure)
- CACI (computer aided cosmetology instrument)
- Guinot Hydradermie Lift

So, in the spirit of research – and let's face it, someone has to do these terrible jobs! – I booked an LIA facial. This treatment, which is a mixture of massage, acupressure and anointing of your face, neck and shoulders with organic unguents, has a significant celebrity following. And I've heard that some of them love these facials so much that they've given up Botox!

I had one in my own home with a very nice therapist who'd been trained by Deborah Mitchell, who devised the treatment. I looked quite glowing as a result, but I honestly can't believe the LIA claim that this treatment retrains the facial muscles – and I certainly didn't detect any lifting of my jaw line.

However, if you love facials, and you feel pampered, relaxed and refreshed as a result, you might want to give it a go.

It's OK to do it naturally

Today we see so many advertisements for plastic surgery and other beauty treatments intended to lift, firm or remove fat that we can easily be carried along and believe that we can't just get old gracefully. Although many of us baby boomers may choose these treatments, many more of us are happy to take care of our skin and body through good diet and exercise, so that we can enjoy our later years looking naturally the best we can.

Botox

Well, what about Botox? Legions of baby boomers are having it. However, film actress Julianne Moore – who is totally gorgeous, by the way – said recently that she had no idea why anyone would have it, because it doesn't make a woman look younger – it just makes her look as though she's had work done.

I agree. I also have a problem with the fact that it's poison. I just can't understand why anyone would want it in her face. But if I were ever tempted to have it done, I'd go to a proper doctor, and that applies to most other rejuvenating procedures that stop short of surgery.

Will they do a good job?

Recently, *Which?* magazine said that our age group is the biggest user of treatments, such as fillers and Botox, but that many of us are going to clinics where the treatment is substandard. So if you are thinking of having one of these treatments, do yourself a big favour and go to a consultant dermatologist who does this kind of work all the time, or to a surgeon on the register of the British Association of Aesthetic Plastic Surgeons (BAAPS).

I'm not saying that all medics are perfect and that every other type of practitioner is rubbish, but if you're treated by a doctor at least you know that he's governed by various professional bodies such as the General Medical Council (GMC), in the UK. You also know that your doctor has completed years of training and fully understands the anatomy and chemistry of the human body.

Thermage

Another treatment that must only be carried out by a doctor is Thermage. It's a procedure that uses radio frequency to tighten up the jowls and sagging facial skin – and you can see what it's like by viewing columnist and TV presenter Carole Malone having it done by Dr Rita Rakus on YouTube.

What happens during the treatment is that the collagen fibres in the skin are heated up. This makes the existing collagen tighten and allegedly promotes further collagen growth. The results are visible immediately, and there's continual improvement for up to six months.

During the session, your face is divided into grids and then radio treatment is applied – stronger in some places than in others. Carole says that the very strongest – which happens last – feels uncomfortable, but not intolerable. She likened it to having a cigarette stubbed out on her face, which didn't sound like much fun, but she's really pleased with the result. She reckons it's saved her from having to consider cosmetic surgery at this point, and is delighted to find that there is genuinely further improvement over a six-month period after the treatment session.

Carole is a no-nonsense individual, and if she says this has improved her appearance, I'm sure it has. I'm seriously tempted to try it – when I've got the money! Prices are around £3,000 for the full face.

Thermage is only administered by medical doctors. And you can find one doing this procedure in your area by going to the Thermage website.

COSMETIC SURGERY

And now the big question: whether or not to go under the knife. Have you ever looked at yourself in the mirror and pulled back the skin on your face in an attempt to picture what you'd look like after a facelift? Go on, admit it! If you haven't already had some work done, I bet you've thought about it. But, like me, you may also have worried about the cost, or that things might go wrong, or even whether it's actually a very ethical thing to do. Also, you may feel anxious, as I have to admit I do, that in some way you may be tempting fate by opting to have surgery that is not absolutely essential.

People often say that what's important in life is to be 'happy in your own skin'. My belief is that it's rather more vital to be happy in your *head*! And I'm convinced that no amount of plastic surgery can turn a miserable person into a happy one. I know several women who have opted for a surgical procedure, but who have then become anxious about some *other* bit of themselves and have then had more surgery. And then more again . . .

Of course, there are baby boomers who just want their breasts lifted – or their tummies tidied up – after having had several children, who will be delighted afterwards and never look back. But when women are psychologically distressed about their lives, it's rather more important that they 'find themselves' in other ways – maybe through counselling – rather than expecting cosmetic surgery to perform miracles.

However, there's no doubt that whatever I have to say on the subject, more and more female baby boomers are seriously contemplating taking the plunge, and if you're one of them, here's what you need to consider.

Experience is essential

For starters, we need to get a really experienced surgeon. Recently, I heard about a doctor who'd been on a short course to learn nose surgery. He then operated – without further training – on the nose of some poor unsuspecting woman, who ended up needing four further operations, which weren't very successful, to try to correct his mistakes.

So, don't be anyone's guinea pig. You want a doc who does your type of operation all the time – not once in a blue moon.

Is your health up to it?

You need to retain your common sense about the whole thing. If you are someone who couldn't have a routine NHS op because doctors would say you need to get your blood pressure and/or your weight down first, you shouldn't even think about cosmetic surgery until you're fitter.

How to choose

If you are relatively fit, but feel distressed by some part of your body, and you can afford surgery, what then? Well, don't pick a surgeon or a company just because they advertise in the back of glossy magazines. In fact, such outfits should probably be at the bottom of your list. There are cosmetic clinics in most cities worldwide where beautiful people swan around in white coats calling themselves 'consultants'. But these are rarely medical experts, and their only function – which they excel at – is to extract large sums of money from your wallet.

They generally hang out in luxurious apartments where the pile of the carpet comes up to your knees, and where the magazine rack in the waiting room is stacked with celebrity magazines full of impossibly perfect and surgically enhanced individuals. But often in such places, if you investigate what the surgeon's qualifications are, you'll discover that although he's a qualified doctor, he's not a specialist plastic surgeon.

Personally, in the UK, I would only go to someone registered with the British Association of Aesthetic Plastic Surgeons (BAAPS). Every one of their surgeons has held a consultant post on the NHS – and some still work in the Health Service.

Furthermore, they're all registered with the General Medical Council (GMC) as specialists in plastic surgery – and you can check this on the GMC website.

Good surgeons are busy and have no need to offer you a free initial consultation. So don't expect one. But despite the fact that you'll have to pay for it, my advice is to visit a couple of different specialists before deciding to go ahead. Cosmetic surgery is a huge step, so, do your homework first.

The most popular cosmetic surgery operations on women in the UK

- Breast augmentation
- Eye-bag removal
- Facelifts
- Breast reduction

Lifting up

Other procedures that are growing in popularity are knee and bum lifts.

The only person I actually know who's had her bottom

lifted is Toyah Willcox. Writing in the *Daily Mail*, she said: 'It's like looking at my bum and thighs as they were 30 years ago.' But then she's in show business, so she has a real reason for doing it. I'm not sure that too many of us are that bothered about our bottoms, or that we'd part with £6,000 just to perk them up a bit. However, I could be wrong.

The thing is that we all have our own anxieties. And when we get a bee in our bonnet about a particular part of our body, it is easier than ever before to get it surgically altered – as long as we've got the dosh.

Travelling for surgery

Talking about money, many women will consider going overseas for surgery, in the hope that it'll be cheaper. Countries such as France and South Africa have some fantastic surgeons – and I certainly know several boomers who've gone to those countries and been thrilled by the results. But there are an awful lot of cosmetic cowboys in the world, and if the deal you're being offered sounds too good to be true, don't touch it.

Quite apart from the quality of the surgery, you also need to remember that you may feel very groggy afterwards and might find it difficult being treated in a country where you don't speak the language. Remember too that you might need aftercare – particularly if things go wrong – and that this could be a big problem once you're flown home.

If you do still want your surgery abroad, the BAAPS

website has a list of international accredited bodies whose members are highly qualified and experienced, and I suggest you pick a surgeon from one of those lists.

Choose the right time

One last thing: it's not a good idea to opt for surgery when you're in the middle of an emotional crisis – such as your husband dying or walking out on you, or you losing your job. You need to deal with your pain and grief first. Cosmetic surgery will not stop you feeling wretched about something that is life-altering and traumatic.

WHERE TO FIND OUT MORE

Ariane Poole: www.arianepoole.com

BAAPS (British Association of Aesthetic Plastic Surgeons): www.baaps.org.uk

Clear Skin UK: www.clearskin-uk.co.uk

Eva Fraser: www.evafraser.com; tel. 020 7937 6616

Fit Flops: www.fitflop.com

GMC (General Medical Council): www.gmc-uk.org

Harley Medical Group: www.harleymedical.co.uk

Marja Putkisto Institute: www.methodputkisto.com; tel. 020 8878 7384

MBT Shoes: http://uk.mbt.com

The Soil Association: www.soilassociation.org

Thermage: www.thermage.co.uk

BOOKS

Naturally Gorgeous, by Charlotte Vøhtz, published by Ebury.
   Charlotte's website, where you can buy her organic products, is: www.greenpeople.co.uk

---

AND FINALLY . . .

I was on holiday recently and saw a woman who was slim
and toned and who had definitely had good cosmetic
surgery. But – she wasn't beautiful. And the reason was
that she had 'dead eyes' and a mean expression, which
ruined the whole effect. There's a moral there! Real beauty
shines out of the eyes – and it comes from being confident in ourselves, and having a zest for life. No beauty
parlour, or cosmetic surgeon, can give you that.

CHAPTER 9

Endless Love

'Love is the answer. But while you're waiting for the answer, sex raises some pretty good questions.' (Woody Allen)

According to Philip Larkin, in his poem 'Annus Mirabilis', sexual intercourse began in 1963! But of course that was far too early for the vast majority of baby boomers, as most of us were still too young – or simply not ready – to relinquish our virginity for some years afterwards. But, we did know that pop stars were all 'at it', and by 1967, it was obvious that there was more to sex than intercourse, because there was some thrilling gossip doing the rounds about 'Mars Bar' parties where the Rolling Stones reputedly ate chocolate treats out of Marianne Faithfull's vagina.

However, most of us could only dream of such exotic practices. For a start, we'd often had awfully basic sex education. My mum had given me a booklet called *The Facts of Life*, which majored on the mating habits of banana flies – so I was none the wiser when I'd finished it. And at school, we had just one lesson on 'human biology', which was mightily embarrassing both for our unmarried woman teacher and for us girls. So we had to depend upon the class sexpert. In Form 4A, ours was Helena Fox. She used to thrill us with her sophisticated lifestyle. I remember her saying, 'And then he put his hand down my blouse . . .' Very exciting, but most of that class didn't even have a boyfriend for a couple of years after that. When we did, loads of us lived in terror of our parents finding out that we were – or wanted to be – sexually active. After all, many mothers were still advising us that wearing trousers was 'unladylike' and that you couldn't use tampons until you were married!

So, flying in the face of all that repression was difficult – and several women I've interviewed told me that they even married the wrong man, rather than have sex outside wedlock and face the wrath of their dads.

Those of us not brave enough to have intercourse usually indulged in 'heavy petting'. That felt safer. After all, we were collectively scared of becoming pregnant, because even though the Pill was becoming available, initially it was only prescribed for married women. It was nearly 1970 before the rest of us could get it.

> ### *You're a baby boomer if . . .*
>
> . . . you remember the panty-girdle. This was another reason for remaining a virgin – it was impenetrable! Many of us wore such a garment – having been told by both our mothers and fashion experts that if we didn't our stomachs would have no muscle tone! What rubbish we swallowed in those days.

THE SEXY 1970S

However, by the 1970s, the sexual revolution was reaching the average teenager and young woman. It became far more acceptable to have sex – and suddenly there was more information available about women's satisfaction and how to achieve it, and many mentions of the clitoris, even if some of us didn't know how to pronounce it.

Cosmopolitan was launched in the UK in 1972, and this gave us a much better idea of what to aim for in the bedroom. Soon afterwards, my husband, Dr David Delvin, started writing a very saucy column in *She* magazine. So, sex was openly on the news-stands and we were all talking about it – and reading everything we could get our hands on.

Several feminist books appeared in the early 1970s too. If you were part of the new 'sisterhood' it was absolutely essential to read Germaine Greer's *The Female Eunuch*. Its frankness took our breath away, with sentences like: 'At all events, a clitoral orgasm with a full c*** is nicer than a clitoral orgasm with an empty one, as far as I can tell at least.'

The clitoris and orgasm: what they said

Sigmund Freud (1856–1939)

Despite his great contribution to psychiatry, Freud knew very little about women's sexual workings. In 1905, he announced that females had two separate types of orgasm – clitoral and vaginal. And he stated that clitoral orgasms were 'immature' or 'infantile'. For many decades this made lots of women feel very inadequate.

Virginia Johnson (b. 1925) and William Masters (1925–2001)

Masters and Johnson studied 382 women who volunteered to climax in their laboratory. In 1966, Masters and Johnson reached the conclusion that *all* female orgasms originated in the clitoris. Unfortunately, they took this to mean that women should be able to reach orgasm from sexual intercourse alone – because the 'in-out' motion of intercourse was supposed to create a tugging effect on the clitoris.

Germaine Greer (b. 1939)

In *The Female Eunuch* (1970), her enormously influential assault on the oppression of women, Greer attacked what she called 'clitoromania', and said: 'Real gratification is not enshrined in a tiny cluster of nerves but in the sexual involvement of the whole person.'

Shere Hite (b.1942)

In 1976, Shere Hite caused worldwide astonishment with her book *The Hite Report on Female Sexuality*. Her survey of 3,000 women revealed that about 70 per cent of women never achieve orgasm through intercourse alone, but that most females can climax easily by means of direct clitoral stimulation – either by themselves or somebody else.

Amazingly, this simple conclusion provoked outrage in America – and even threats to her life. The hostility was so great that she eventually renounced her US citizenship and went to live permanently in Europe.

The 1970s

As the 1970s wore on they 'swung' much more than the 1960s ever had. Far more unmarried people were having sex all over the place. And young married couples, too, often adopted racy lifestyles behind their net curtains. They held wine and cheese parties where lots of extra-marital canoodling went on. And in some of the most sedate of suburbs, 'wife-swapping' was rife.

The knock-on effect

It was supposed to be great, but many marriages crumbled quicker than freshly baked cookies. Others lasted, for a while, but I don't know any couple living that 'open marriage' lifestyle who stayed together long term – although a few may have done.

It certainly wasn't unbridled fun. Lots of people felt distressed and jealous at these goings on – even though it was uncool to show it. Somehow, though, we survived all this turbulence. Most of us settled down, and thankfully the reforms in divorce meant that those of us who'd made bad choices the first time round could free ourselves to try again.

So what's our attitude to sex now?

Here we are then — all these years later. What do we feel about sex now? In my survey of baby boomers:

- 26 per cent of women were definitely up for sex.
- 29 per cent said they quite liked it.
- 21 per cent didn't care for it much.
- 6 per cent answered that they didn't like it at all.
- And 16 per cent said they might enjoy it if they got a new partner!

We have been sexual beings in a way our mothers mostly were not, and many of us are still looking for physical satisfaction as well as love. Unfortunately, just as our early sexual lives were often pretty uncertain and unsettled, mid life throws up plenty of challenges too.

LIVENING UP A LONG-TERM RELATIONSHIP

Often — and rather gloriously — a long-term relationship becomes closer and warmer with age. If we're lucky, the kids are off our hands and we may realise just how much we value the companionship our partner offers. Sex sometimes improves too. It might not have the breathless passion of our earliest days, but many women report it as being enjoyable, reassuring and rewarding – and an essential part of a genuinely authentic loving relationship.

And there is good research to show that couples who are affectionate, tactile and sexual with each other have oodles of the bonding hormone called oxytocin racing around their bloodstreams, and far less of the stress hormone called cortisol. So, being in a loving and sexual relationship is a healthy place to be.

New tricks

Sadly, however, many boomers feel that sex has gone stale. And when that happens, they wonder if it's possible to spice things up – without feeling silly. One client said to me: 'Don't suggest I dress up in a French maid's outfit or lie around wearing nothing but a basque and a come-hither look. I couldn't possibly do it!' Who can blame her? It's hard to suddenly be a vamp, when you've been sharing the same bed with your partner for 30 years and sex has become perfunctory.

If this sounds like you, my suggestion is that you liven up your mind, which – after all – is a woman's key erogenous zone. Try talking to each other in bed about what turns you on. Let your imagination run wild. Frankly, most fantasies would cause havoc if they were acted out in real life, so don't actually invite the beautiful young divorcée next door to join you; just pretend!

Alternatively, make up sex stories, or read some. We women tend to be much more stimulated by the written word than by pictures. (Men of course are usually the opposite, which accounts for the huge increase in Internet porn.) So we're often turned on by erotic literature – rather than by watching pneumatic lovelies simulating climaxes – and can create deliciously arousing pictures in our heads while reading or being read to.

You can find suitable books on the Passion8 and Sh! websites – and in high street bookshops, if you're feeling brave enough to buy them there.

Also, you can download short stories from a website called Literotica. Beware though, these are written by amateurs – so don't expect perfect prose! And they are really explicit, so don't go there if you're easily shocked.

I CAN'T GET NO SATISFACTION

For some women, one of their mid-life challenges is to find enjoyment in sex. Maybe they feel they've missed out on sexual satisfaction – and they'd now like to experience it. And why not? One of the greatest things about sex is that it's never too late to turn yourself on to it.

In 1995, my husband and I wrote a book called *The Big 'O'*. Our research for it showed that women of all ages can achieve climaxes – and that some managed it for the first time well into mid life.

A recent Danish study conducted by Pia Struck found much the same thing. She took 500 'chronic anorgasmic women' and gave them a course of group therapy and sex education – as well as providing them all with clitoral vibrators. At the end of the study, 465 patients (93 per cent) were able to climax in the presence of the therapist. And just as many post-menopausal women achieved success as their younger counterparts. This is heartening news for baby boomers who have found climaxing difficult.

Most women who learn to orgasm later in life do it through masturbation. Fortunately, far fewer women feel guilty about masturbation than ever before. This is great – because a bit of DIY activity can be marvellous. In fact, it's the safest and most reliable method of sex that there is. And it should be a delicious experience – not something furtive or hurried.

Achieving satisfaction

For variety, many women buy erotica or sex toys. Vibrators nowadays are not the absurd pink plastic phallus monstrosities of days gone by. There are lovely designer ones. Sex expert Julia Cole co-designed a range called Emotional Bliss. And there are good online sex shops such as Passion8 and Sh! that sell really classy vibes.

Some women, of course, find that a new partner does the trick and that although they never climaxed with their previous spouse, they are able to feel liberated, sexy and adventurous with a different guy.

Alas, if you've always faked it, it is much harder to learn how to orgasm with your long-term partner – and terribly hard to broach the subject if you'd like things to improve. I had a client who tried to have this conversation with her husband of 25 years. Instead of being helpful, he told her not to be silly and said that he'd have known if she'd been pretending all that time. What arrogance!

Needless to say, that relationship never recovered. My client has stayed with her husband but they no longer have sex – and she now takes younger lovers, and orgasms with them.

The very good news is that these days there is a lot of help around for women who find climaxing difficult. If you fancy a trip to Denmark, you can sign up for a course with the Orgasm Academy. Relationship therapy in the UK – or elsewhere – can also help. And there are loads of books on the subject, including a brilliant one by Rachel Swift, called *How to Have an Orgasm . . . As Often as You Want: Life Changing Secrets for Women and their Partners*. Plus, there are DVDs and books by sex-guru Betty Dodson, whose methods have helped women worldwide to ring that elusive bell.

And on the Netdoctor website, there are masses of articles on all sorts of sex and relationship problems – including one on achieving orgasm.

MID-LIFE RELATIONSHIP CHALLENGES

Learning how to become more orgasmic can be the most fantastic experience for a woman who's previously found it difficult. But it is only one of the challenges we face in mid life. In fact, this time of our lives is a pretty hazardous one for our relationships. After all, this is a period of massive transition. Children leave home. Partners retire – often before us. People get ill. Others worry that they have missed out on great sex – or great loving – and want to remedy that before it's too late.

If he leaves you

The traditional scenario of a man having a mid-life crisis and riding off into the sunset with his young secretary is far from the only danger to a marriage nowadays. Of course, it does still happen. And for a woman to be brutally discarded by her husband just at a time when she thought her life was sorted forever is a truly dreadful experience. If you have recently been left by a long-term partner, my best advice is to lean on your friends and family and let them look after you, just as they would if you were physically ill.

Also, do visit the So You've Been Dumped website, which has helped countless people. If you need counselling, try Relate or find a private therapist through the British Association for Sexual and Relationship Therapy (BASRT).

Feeling you've had enough

Nowadays, it's just as common for the fairer sex to get itchy feet in mid life. And mostly they feel far more confident than their mothers ever were about pulling the plug on a redundant relationship.

One client told me how her marriage had ended. Her last child had flown the nest, and to celebrate – and in a bid to rekindle some romance – she and her husband had booked a very expensive holiday in the Seychelles.

Sadly, each night over dinner in their fabulously romantic location, they'd found that they were strangers, with nothing to say to each other. When they came home, she asked for a divorce. Ten years on, I asked this former client if she had any regrets about having split up with her husband.

'None,' she said. She also said that she doesn't envy her girlfriends who are in marriages with men of the same age or older. 'The guys all seem to be giving up – and getting ill, or needing surgery – while the women are fizzing with enthusiasm and still energetic and ambitious to do all sorts of things.'

This energy and enthusiasm can often manifest itself in the bedroom.

Many women of our age now have time – and the inclination – for more love-making. But often they yearn for something rather more sensuous than the stuff that's been on the menu thus far. The trouble is that sometimes a spouse is set in his ways and thinks that the only 'proper sex' is intercourse. This can lead to dissatisfaction and arguments. At this stage the wife often literally takes matters into her own hands and buys a vibrator. She may even go looking for a lover – who, by the way, is not always male.

Mid-life changes

Recently, I spoke about the failure rate of marriages in mid life with three of Britain's top relationships counsellors: Julia Cole, Denise Knowles and Paula Hall. Julia says that today's mid-life woman is much less likely than her mother to settle for what she has. But she says that if a woman plucks up courage to talk to her husband about improving their relationship in and out of bed, he's often bemused because he may well think that everything's fine. And he'll say 'helpful' things like: 'Nothing's changed, it's always been like this.'

Denise Knowles says that female baby boomers have

often grown in confidence. Maybe they didn't work when their kids were small, but now they find themselves running businesses or occupying senior positions in big companies. But just at the point when they've found their feet – and are feeling confident and adventurous in and out of bed – their partners want a quiet life, or may even be experiencing sexual difficulties.

Paula Hall says, 'With time, looks and agility running out, many women feel they have to make a speedy decision about whether or not their current relationship will work, or whether they should get out there on the dating market asap while they've still got a chance.'

So, these are testing times.

Fears for the future

Another problem I've encountered with clients is their dread of ending up as a nursemaid. Obviously, if you are deeply in love with your partner, and he becomes seriously ill, you will take on his care because it wouldn't occur to you not to look after him. But if the relationship is already rocky, then this is a different situation entirely.

A teacher said to me, 'I'm sitting on a health time-bomb. My husband and I don't get on and he's the sort of guy who thinks that salad is for rabbits and exercise is for fools. He hasn't looked after himself at all. I need to leave now. If I wait till he's had a stroke, it'll be too late.'

Retirement – his or yours – is another crunch time. A client who runs her own PR agency is married to a man who's changed dramatically since retiring from his top-executive job: all he wants to do is lie around in his dressing-gown watching Sky Sports.

'It's unbelievably dreadful,' she told me.

'Is it so bad you're considering divorce?' I asked.

'It's so bad, I'm considering murder!' she retorted.

That couple worked things out eventually. And many men and women do adjust and compromise – just as they have at earlier times in their relationship. But, for some, retirement is a step too far.

Big birthdays or anniversaries can be dangerous times too. If you find that you're dreading celebrating your silver wedding because it feels like a sham, you may need to start asking yourself whether you want your marriage to continue into old age.

Affairs

Another major mid-life challenge occurs when one of the couple has had an affair and confesses to it, or gets found out. Of course, it's very dramatic and traumatic if a divorce results. But, quite commonly, the straying partner comes to the conclusion that the new romance can't replace – or compensate for – the infrastructure that the marriage provides. So, it's not just sex or love that keeps people at home. They may stay in the marriage because they like their in-laws and hate the thought of missing out on those extended family gatherings at Christmas, birthdays and anniversaries.

Some people give up on an affair because they fear their children's hostility if they don't. Many decide that no new love is worth the inevitable expense of divorce.

However, rebuilding a marriage after an affair is never easy. A marital partner may forgive but find it impossible to forget. The 'guilty' partner may want to stop talking about why he or she was unfaithful, but the 'innocent' one may need to keep talking about it to make some sense of it all. This can cause friction.

The best chance a couple has of staying together after an affair is when they both accept some responsibility for the state of their relationship prior to it. But if the so-called innocent party maintains that he or she was perfect and that the guilty partner was a total rat, there is little hope for reconciliation.

Winding down – or up

Another big mid-life challenge is when one partner wants to retire in a conventional sense and just potter around and wind down, and the other partner – usually the woman – has all sorts of adventurous plans for travel and study and maybe for starting up a new business. Can a relationship accommodate such different attitudes? Undoubtedly it can, but it's not easy – and if it is to survive, then the couple really need to communicate about what each of them hopes for over the next decade or so.

If real love and trust exists between them, then it may be possible for one partner to go and volunteer in Bolivia, or travel to Venice with a friend, or embark upon a university degree – especially if the other partner has some definite plans too. Then, each spouse can support the other emotionally, albeit from a distance.

But, if the less adventurous partner is miserable and becomes negative and possessive or pathetic, it can be hard to hold things together. Obviously, couples whose expectations of the next few decades are similar – and who are still in love and lust – are far better placed to sustain their relationships than couples who want very different things.

But if you're someone who is ambitious and active, and you are living with someone who is not, then you have to weigh up all your options. Will you be more unhappy if you disappoint yourself and give up your dreams, and opt not to rock the boat, than if you pursue your plans and risk divorce?

There are some tough decisions to be made.

IT'S NOW OR NEVER – TO SPLIT OR NOT

We probably all know women who have divorced and who relish their freedom and look vital and energised and happy. But there are plenty of others who massively regret the end of the marriage. The harsh truth is that life after divorce is often not all it's cracked up to be. Most women are financially worse off after divorce and masses of them do not find Mr Right.

In fact, some realise all too late that boring old Ben, or dull old Derek, was actually a very decent man. And they are shattered when their previously unexciting husbands are snapped up by other women who think they are gorgeous!

However, plenty of boomers do want out of their marriages, and although the divorce rate is falling in general, it's rising in our age group – and in older ones too. One law firm told me that their oldest divorcée had been 92! And this is not just a British phenomenon. It's happening elsewhere in the Western world – Switzerland, for example, where women feel more confident about being on their own.

But the divorce of a long-term couple does have a huge and unsettling impact on the whole family – including grown-up children and grandchildren. It alters the family fabric and dynamic, which may never recover. So, this is one of the hugest decisions you are ever going to make. Are you going to stay, or go?

I would certainly say that if a woman is in a violent

marriage, she should definitely end it. But most relationship difficulties are less clear-cut. So ask your friends who
have left their partners what they've experienced and
whether they have regrets. Also, ask yourself the following
questions:

1 Does my partner make me laugh?
2 Do we still have lots in common?
3 Do I love him?
4 Does he love me?
5 Do I enjoy having sex with him?
6 Does he make me feel better about myself?
7 Does he praise and encourage me?
8 Is he kind to me?
9 Would I miss all the happy extended family
   occasions that we have?

If you answer 'no' far more than 'yes' you may begin to
feel that your relationship has passed its sell-by date.

Frankly, if you dread going home after work, or feel
criticised or put down, or stifled or unloved, then you're
not getting the sustenance, and bonding and companionship that most people value in a good marriage.

Splitting up – whether or not it involves divorce – is
miserable at any age. But if you are going to go, it's probably better that you cut loose sooner rather than later.
There are various websites that offer useful information –
including On Divorce and Wikivorce. And if you are ending
a relationship, my strong suggestion is that you should both
engage lawyers from the organisation called Resolution,

who are committed to helping couples part with the minimum of acrimony.

DATING AGAIN

How will your romantic life be after the split? Lots of women in my survey put 'getting a new man' at the top of their wish-list. But if you've recently left a relationship, you may worry that you're too old to have another one. Nerves are understandable, but try not to underestimate your charms. The chances are that celebrities such as Felicity Kendal, Joanna Lumley and Helen Mirren are older than you and yet they frequently turn up on men's fantasy lists.

Of course, lots of us agonise that we're not in the shape we once were. Loads of women worry about their less-than-firm tummy. But are men bothered? Not usually. It's the sisterhood who go, 'Bloody hell — look at the stomach on that!'

We worry about cellulite too. But most guys don't even know what it is. What most of them want is a warm smile, welcoming arms and an enthusiasm for lovemaking. And I bet you can provide that.

So, how can you find someone new? Well, be open to novel experiences. After all, you no longer need to find someone your mother will approve of, or who fits your blueprint of the 'perfect dad'. If you're lucky, you may know him already. Often once we're free, we find that someone we've known for ages has always fancied us.

Widening your net

Girlfriends will probably also be trying to match-make you with their divorced brothers and so on. But if no one in your immediate circle seems suitable, then why not try Lonely Hearts ads and Internet dating?

If you opt for the dating page in the newspaper you generally read, you should find that you have something in common — politically at least — with the men advertising there. By the way, usually the newspaper prints a code of conduct and some sensible rules for when you arrange a first meeting. Responsible sites on the Internet do that too. In case you're worried, Internet dating is seen as trendy these days — and not at all sad. However, lecturer Lorna Meadows says that a lot of 50-plus men on Internet sites are boring and unsexy and that she had to 'kiss a lot of toads' before she found her current, lovely partner.

If you're gay — and around five per cent of us are — there are specialist magazines where you might find love, but plenty of mainstream newspapers and Internet sites are catering for you too.

Maybe, on the other hand, you're merely 'bi-curious'; the new methods of dating may help you to explore what you're curious about.

Match.com is the market leader in Internet dating — and their users include vast quantities of 'second-time rounders'. Another popular site is Plenty of Fish.com. And if you're over 50, there's Saga Connections.

It won't all be plain sailing. One of my girlfriends thought she'd found someone suitable in the paper, so they arranged to meet. The first time he cancelled because he had a cold. The next time he couldn't come because his car broke down. A third time he was having trouble with his claustrophobia . . .

There wasn't a fourth time!

SEX WITH SOMEONE NEW

If you do find someone you like and things hot up, how is the sex going to be?

Well, for many women – particularly those whose previous romance left lots to be desired in the bedroom department – it's a wonderfully passionate and liberating experience. Sexual taste buds are awakened and unfulfilled desires and fantasies come to the fore.

Although it's natural to feel anxious, most of us in new sexual situations do better this time around in expressing our wants and needs. By the way, lots of women who are worried about exposing what they see as 'wobbly bodies' feel better if they make love by candlelight!

Different adventures

The team at the sex shop Sh! tell me that mid-life women in new relationships are great customers. They buy loads of gadgets and want to try everything – including 'bottom-play'.

The bottom has a plenteous supply of nerve endings and can be a source of enormous pleasure. But the fact is that many of us do not like – or do not want to try – anal intercourse with a man, because it can really hurt. Of course through the ages, women have always agreed to please their guys in this way – from time to time – even if it's not their cup of tea. Some offer it as a birthday treat!

But I'm told that newly in-love-and-lust women are keen to buy anal vibrators – which deliver the good sensations without the discomfort. One word of caution: don't use an ordinary vibrator for this activity. It can get lost! You need a special one that has a kind of shelf at the end: this stops the gadget disappearing up inside you and lodging itself in your intestines. Imagine the embarrassment of going to A & E with your insides buzzing!

DOWNSIDES TO NEW SEX

Unfortunately, sometimes our bodies let us down just when we're having the best sex of our lives. Vaginal dryness is the main difficulty. We just have to accept that we're not as copious in our production of natural lubrication as we once were. Women on HRT shouldn't have this problem, but the rest of us often do.

However, sex shops sell lovely lubrications that should suit – such as Liquid Silk, Wet and Pjur. And don't feel ashamed that you need this bit of help. The Sh! team tell me that it's only heterosexual women who feel uneasy about needing lubricant. Apparently, lesbians have no compunction about buying it by the bucket-load!

If things don't improve, talk to your doctor about getting some hormone cream. This can also help if you're unlucky enough to keep getting cystitis – which does, alas, become fairly common in our age group. If it's a problem for you, take a look at Angela Kilmartin's website. You might also want to get one of her excellent books on cystitis.

Angela knows more about cystitis than the vast majority of doctors – having suffered so badly from the condition in her twenties that she had to abandon a promising operatic career. Her methods for stopping a painful attack of cystitis have helped women worldwide for decades.

Pelvic floor exercises (PFEs)

If you've had babies, you probably learned how to do PFEs decades ago. But we should all still do them, because we need good pelvic muscle tone if we're going to continue to enjoy sex – and avoid incontinence.

Lots of women feel that they've let things go in this department. A friend of mine decided to remedy the situation by buying an exerciser called a vaginal dumbbell. Unfortunately, the first time she inserted it, her internal muscles were so slack that it dropped out and broke her toe!

The usual way to do PFEs is to pull in your abdomen from the tummy button and then draw up your pelvic muscles as if you're trying to stop yourself from peeing. You hold this position for a count of ten, and then relax for ten seconds. To make any real difference you need to do at least ten repetitions, ten times a day for several months.

If you're anything like me, you do your PFEs somewhat haphazardly – like when you're waiting in the bus queue. And you're probably not doing them often enough to see much improvement.

For more consistent results you could treat yourself to an electronic Kegel Exerciser. You can get one from the Passion8 website, by clicking on 'For Women' and then clicking on 'Pelvic Health'. Stephanie Taylor, who founded the company, says that they are 'walking off the shelves'.

Safe sex

Another downside to new sex is the possibility that you'll catch something nasty. Various surveys have shown that as an age group we're not clued up enough about sexual infection and that when we find some new dishy partner it doesn't occur to us that he might be carrying a sexually transmitted disease.

So, make sure your man uses a condom. You might find it embarrassing to address this with him. But it's far better to deal with those uncomfortable feelings than end up with something horrid – like chlamydia, genital warts or herpes – or even HIV, syphilis or gonorrhoea.

Unfortunately, many mid-life men are reluctant to use a condom, because they're anxious that putting one on will make them go limp. But if you want to be safe, you need to insist. One way to make a guy feel more secure about his erection is for you to put the condom on him – stroking him as you do so. Hopefully, this will be exciting for him and the whole experience won't fall flat!

ALTERNATIVE SEX AND LOVING

Maybe you're thinking that it would be fun to join the increasing number of female celebrities who are swinging from the chandeliers twice nightly with a younger bloke. Most women pick guys who are only up to about 12 years younger than them. However, some females do have a penchant for much younger lads. If this is you, take a look at Toyboy.com. I suspect that mostly – in exchange for sex – you'll always end up paying for dinner! But you might not mind that.

Some women also go in for sex tourism – which basically means going on holiday with the intention of finding a young lover among the locals. If you think this sounds exciting, do practise safe sex, and try to make sure that you don't discard your common sense along with your inhibitions. Your experience is unlikely to lead to true and lasting love. Hopefully, you'll have a good time – but he will probably expect money. That's how it is.

Of course, in many countries of the world, including the UK, you can pay for sex with escorts. I've met a few of these guys on TV programmes, and I have to say that mostly they seem hunky, but rather dim. So don't expect great conversation!

Nowadays, some women, as well as men, join organisations that promise to deliver sex without emotional hassle. Illicit Encounters is one of those and they have over 8,000 women members aged between 45 and 65. I doubt if many of us would actually consider looking for excitement in such a calculated way. But I can see that if a woman's long-term relationship is fine – apart from the sex – then this could be some kind of an answer.

Of course, affairs where people meet up by accident or at work will continue to happen. In fact, I'm sure there is far more extracurricular activity going on in our generation than there was in our mums' time – mostly because we have far more opportunities to meet men.

And some affairs have gone on for decades. I know of several instances where a couple – both married – have worked together and fallen in love, and where those affairs have been true love matches and far more sustaining than either legitimate relationship.

Usually, such people have stayed married for the sake of their families. But what happens to these 'soulmate' affairs when the couple reach retirement? Once the opportunity to meet is severely curtailed, there is usually a lot of heartache. Should they now each leave their marriages and make that break they've longed for? Or do the ties of home – the friendship and companionship with the marital partner and the pull of the kids – mean that the affair has finally to end?

Whatever happens, it's very painful for someone.

WHERE TO FIND OUT MORE

BASRT (British Association For Sexual and Relationship Therapy): www.basrt.org.uk

Betty Dodson: www.bettydodson.com. (Unless you live in America, it may be easier to buy her books and DVDs from Amazon.)

Julia Cole (Emotional Bliss): www.emotionalbliss.co.uk

Paula Hall: www.paulahall.co.uk
Illicit Encounters: www.illicitencounters.co.uk
Denise Knowles: 01604 408686
Literotica: www.literotica.com
Netdoctor: www.netdoctor.co.uk/sex_relationships
On Divorce: www.ondivorce.co.uk
Orgasm Academy: www.orgasmacademy.eu
Passion8: www.passion8.com
Plenty of Fish: www.plentyoffish.com
Relate: www.relate.org.uk
Resolution: www.resolution.org.uk
Saga Dating: www.saga.co.uk/connections
Sh!: www.sh-womenstore.co.uk
So You've Been Dumped: www.soyouvebeendumped.co.uk
Toyboys: www.toyboy.com
Wikivorce: www.wikivorce.com

BOOKS

How to Have an Orgasm . . . As Often as You Want: Life Changing Secrets for Women and their Partners, by Rachel Swift, published by Marlowe and Co.

The Patient's Encyclopaedia of Urinary Tract Infection, Sexual Cystitis and Interstitial Cystitis, by Angela Kilmartin, published by New Century Press; see also: www.angelakilmartin.com

---

LOOKING FORWARD

So, all in all it seems likely that many of us might have quite unconventional sex lives as we grow older. Some of us will have great sex within marriage. Others will find pleasure outside it. And plenty of us will be doing something so secretive than even our best friends don't know about it.

We're still doing it 'our way' after all these years!

CHAPTER 10

With a Little Help From My Friends

'Friends are God's apology for relations.' (Hugh Kingsmill)

Thank God for mates. When you have a bad day, or a row with your children, or your demented mother is driving you crazy, or you're feeling put upon, you can always 'phone a friend'.

Friendships have been fantastically important to us baby boomers. And as we get older they will remain vital to us – particularly as lots of us are single, or likely to become so. We will also turn to our friends for companionship if, for example, we want to travel but our men want to stay at home. We may even have plans to live with our pals – particularly if our money doesn't look like stretching as far as we once thought it might.

We have made friends throughout our lives – and from all over the UK and beyond. In fact we were the first generation of women who had the chance to do so, which may be one reason why we value our friendships so much.

OUR FRIENDSHIP NETWORKS

Of course most of us don't have as big a social circle as today's 20- and 30-somethings: I don't suppose any of us claim to have – or want – 347 friends on Facebook! But significantly, we're the first group of females to believe that our friends are just as important as our families – or even more so.

So, how and why did that happen? Well, it's mostly been about our opportunities. Some of these opportunities have distanced us from our relatives, so we've naturally gravitated towards the mates who've shared similar experiences. For example, those of us who were lucky enough to go to university or college have kept in touch with friends from that time – of both genders.

∿ Case Study: Heather and Nigel ∿

An extraordinary example of such 'student' friendships is the one enjoyed by leading astronomers and broadcasters Heather Couper and Nigel Henbest. Although they've never been a romantic couple, they've not only worked together since university – and formed their own media company – but they have always lived in the same house too.

Heather says,

> *As we specialise in the same subjects and have always worked together doing what we enjoy, we've regarded*

ourselves as 'students forever'. We've never really grown up, I suppose. And I love that.

Big changes from something small

Another huge difference in our friendships happened because of the Pill. It's hard for younger people today to grasp how this one invention transformed women's lives. It was also a further nail in the coffin of our similarities with our own mothers, and another reason why we bonded with our female friends – because they too were living through these monumental changes.

Heather Couper was delighted to take advantage of the new science, which allowed her to avoid parenthood. She wasn't alone. Masses of us put our careers first, and either sought to remain childless or never got round to being mothers.

Friendships through the kids – and beyond

But the majority of us did have children, and that opened up opportunities for more traditional friendships with other mums. However, these friendships were not as key as they might have been had we stayed at home long term, which we didn't.

Our mothers, on the other hand, were often housewives whose friends were limited to neighbours, other mums at the school gates and people who went to the same church.

∼ Case Study: Janet ∼

Broadcaster and former *Blue Peter* presenter, Janet Ellis, says,

> *I have a network of girlfriends. My mum never had anything like that. As I've always worked, most of my friends have started as colleagues. And I've tended to keep one really good one from every period of my life – from drama school through to the present day. We've been able to meet so many people in ways that were simply not open to our mothers.*

So, for us baby boomers, colleagues are a huge component of our social circle. Another difference compared with women of previous generations is that we've always had male as well as female friends: men who were never lovers, but just mates. Plenty of us have also had male gay friends: something else that our mums rarely experienced.

And of course – thanks to working and moving around the country, pursuing various interests and taking courses, and so on – we've had oodles of opportunities to make friends from different generations. I think it's great that nowadays we can have pals who are positive babes compared to us.

So, we have plenty of friends – of all kinds and ages. And they've been collected along the way as our lives have progressed. In other words, they're a right mixture! But then, so are we.

My little friend, Vittoria

One of my loveliest friendships is with someone I met when I was 28, and she was seven! At the time, I was a not-very-good actress and singer, playing the title role in a tatty production of *The Sleeping Beauty*. After the show one afternoon, a sweet little girl came backstage. She was gratifyingly bowled over by the magic of her first visit to a theatre. In fact, she wrote to me afterwards describing how beautiful it was. And that began years of letter writing and friendship.

Fast-forwarding to today, she is a successful writer, and we're still friends – despite my having told her recently how awful that panto was, thus treading all over her childhood memories and dreams!

TEND AND BEFRIEND

Women have always been good at grouping together for support. Some psychologists think this dates from prehistory when we were living in tribes. They believe that our response to any kind of threat was to 'tend and befriend'. This makes perfect sense. After all, the 'fight or flight' response – which is what most of us think of in terms of reacting to danger – was not really possible for women in the past, because they were generally either pregnant or encumbered by small children, or both. So, because they couldn't run or fight, their reaction to threat was to support each other.

It's important for us to recognise that this trait is part of our make up, and that it will be useful over the next few decades. Most of us have a large circle of friends and we can use this network to sustain and care for each other in the coming years.

But what is a friend?

Maybe at this point it would be useful to establish what we mean by 'a friend'. At school, it was common to have a 'best friend' and maybe one or two lesser ones. Some of us have kept to that format. Others of us – especially if we've lived all over the country and had several different jobs – have a considerably larger circle of mates.

In my questionnaire, I asked how many friends each respondent had. The average number was nine.

Some women had dozens of pals and others only a couple. So what became clear is that we define friendship in different ways. For those baby boomers who claim only a modest number of friends, real friendship is obviously something very precious, intimate and long term. Anyone who is not quite 'special enough' is not deemed a friend, but a colleague or an acquaintance.

But women who have 50 friends clearly define friendship more loosely. They see their various mates as fulfilling a wide variety of functions. In other words, they're not all crucial or long term – some are just fun.

These differences set me thinking about what friendship means to me, and I came to the conclusion that, in my case, a friend is someone who:

- I like a lot, even if the contact with that individual is much more commonly by email/phone than in person.
- I'm always pleased to be in contact with – and feel that he/she is pleased to be in touch with me too.
- I've shared personal details and confidences with.
- I can laugh with.
- Has similar interests and attitudes – but not necessarily identical ones.
- I could turn to if I needed comfort or help.
- I would be pleased to help if they were in trouble of any kind.

ARE YOU GETTING ENOUGH?

You might want to come up with your own list of conditions of friendship: it's quite useful, particularly if you're working out whether your network of friends is sufficient. The chances are that at the moment – and particularly if you're still working – you feel you've got plenty of mates, just not enough time to see them all! And finding time is usually even more difficult if you are in a close and loving relationship.

As someone who has been virtually joined at the hip to Lovely Husband for the past 23 years, I understand what it is to have a partner who's also a best mate – and I know that it can be awfully difficult to keep in contact with friends as much as you want, while also finding enough time to be with your partner.

However, in my job as a therapist, I see countless women who had believed themselves to be romantically sorted, but who now find themselves alone. And it's often terribly hard for them to recover from their broken hearts if they've failed to keep up with their pals during that now extinct relationship.

And even if our romances do continue to go swimmingly, we have to face the fact that unless we and our partners are simultaneously wiped out in a plane or car crash, one of us is bound to outlive the other. And then what?

Frankly, if we haven't put effort into nurturing our friendships, we could end up isolated and lonely.

Losing some of our friends

Another unpleasant truth is that some of our friends are going to die. You may already have learned the hard way that not everyone in your social circle is going to have the luxury of worrying about old age.

Unfortunately, over the next 20 years, unless we're extraordinarily lucky, more bad things will happen to good friends. Also, there's no doubt that as we get older we may want to drop those pals who drone on about their illnesses, or who seem to be embracing a kind of middle or old age that doesn't sit well with our view of things.

So, although it might seem calculating, we need to accept that unless we keep topping up our pool of friends, it's likely to evaporate rather alarmingly.

So do we really have enough?

We baby boomers have always tended to have plenty of friends. So there's no reason for us to become isolated, which is great, because that way we'll have a good chance of avoiding the depression that is rife in solitary older people.

However, it will get harder to keep up with mates as we grow older, and we will lose some – so we need to make an effort to maintain a sizeable number of friends for the future.

FRIENDS FOR THE FUTURE

Like most of us who've kept fit and been lucky enough not to get any serious illnesses, I don't feel I've altered much physically or mentally in the last 30 years. But even with my baby-boomer invincibility, I have to concede that this happy state of affairs won't last indefinitely, and that in the next 30 years there are bound to be loads of changes.

However, it's difficult to anticipate how our thinking may change as the years go by. We can't yet know what we might think, feel and need if we become infirm, less capable, a bit dotty and maybe immobile. And it's also hard to ponder the question of what sort of friends we might want.

When I've discussed with fellow baby boomers what our main reasons might be for needing our mates in the future, I've been struck by the number of women who worry how they'll fare if they end up living alone.

Some have told me how they have older friends living by themselves, who've become self-obsessed, garrulous and plain potty, and how they're determined not to follow suit.

Old and new friends, new pursuits

So maybe we should give a little thought to what our future friendship needs might be – and put some building blocks in place – so that when we are much older than we can currently imagine, it won't be horrible. Maybe we have to rethink what we'll do with friends, and what we'll be able to offer them. Perhaps at the moment, we mostly go out to restaurants or pubs with them – or to the theatre. In time, we'll probably have less cash to splash around, so it could be useful to start working out now how we can continue to have fun with friends without spending too much.

Obviously, in the UK, there is free admission to most museums. We have plenty of parks to walk in too. But it could also be great to entertain more at home. It doesn't have to be too ambitious: one of you cooks a simple main course, another brings a pudding, and another a bottle of wine. Apart from chatting, you can always make a TV programme into an event – whether you're into sport or the soaps, *The Eurovision Song Contest* or films.

You may also have found – as I have – that Sky Arts Two programmes now include wonderful world-class operas, ballets and concerts. Dressing up as if you're going to the opera – but staying at home with good mates and a simple supper – could be a cheap and convivial way to spend an evening.

We just need to get our heads around the idea that being with our mates needn't cost a lot.

REVIEWING THE FRIENDS WE HAVE

As a first step in ensuring that you have sufficient friends for now, and the future, why not review what you have?

Do you like your current bunch of mates? Are you in regular contact with the ones you really value? Or are there loads of hangers-on you wish would just go away?

In Janet Street Porter's book *Life's Too F***ing Short*, she writes, 'Ruthlessly analyse your address book, chuck out people you haven't seen for two years. Start a new book, and only put in the people you really want to see.' She also suggests editing out 'old work colleagues, neighbours from when we were growing up, worthy people, boring people and men we may have slept with out of pity!'

This might sound brutal, but if we're to have time for those individuals we genuinely want to see, we may need to do some pruning.

Who should stay, and who should go?

What most of us really, really want is to be surrounded by mates who make us feel good: those people we're always pleased to see – because they lift our mood and give us energy. So are you seeing enough of those? Or are you seeing too much of those you could live without?

Doctors and therapists often talk about 'heart-sink' patients. These are the ones who make you groan when you realise they're next on your list of patients. *Oh God*, you think. *Not her.* They're always negative – despite your best efforts. And whatever you suggest, they quickly tell you, 'I've tried that,' or 'Oh no, that wouldn't work for me.' Well, sometimes we have heart-sink friends. But should we keep them?

Maybe our decision will depend upon whether their negativity is well entrenched, or just temporary. But can someone be a true friend if you keep thinking: *I really ought to get in touch, but I don't want to*? Probably not.

DRAWING UP A FRIENDSHIP LIST

So, why not make a friendship inventory? Use your own set of rules about what you think a real friend should be – and then go through your email contacts and address book, and find how many of them measure up to what you want. I've just done my own list – and this is what I found:

- I have 32 friends.
- The youngest is in his twenties.
- The oldest three are in their eighties.
- Most of the others are baby boomers.
- Twenty-two are my friends – and the rest I share jointly with my husband.
- One dates from my school days, and four from college.
- The vast majority are, or have been, work colleagues.
- A third of them are men.

It was really illuminating to see which of all my colleagues and acquaintances I valued enough to call 'friend'. It's helped me to understand who really matters. And I now have plans to meet some individuals very much more – and some a bit less. Let's hope that those I've put at the top of my list are keen to have me at the top of theirs!

Women and friendships

A recent study carried out by the Research Centre for Socio-Cultural Change at the University of Manchester found that:

- Women see friendship as a means of expressing themselves and forming their identity, whereas men look at relationships in a self-seeking way, as in 'What's in it for me?'

- Friendship between women seems to be much deeper and more moral than men's friendships. The researchers found that 'It's about the relationship itself rather than what they can get out of it.'

- Women tend to keep their friends through thick and thin, across geography and social mobility.

CATCHING UP WITH OLD FRIENDS

One of the strangest aspects of getting older is how we often crave companionship with the people we've known the longest. Irvin Yalom, the distinguished writer and psychotherapist, who is now in his late seventies, says that as he ages, 'events from long ago pull at me'. In a recent article, he described how 'I find the past ever more with me.' This has led him to revisit childhood haunts and attend school reunions where he describes himself as being 'more moved than I used to be'.

He feels that there's something intrinsic in us – as we contemplate whatever time there is left to us – to seek out some of the people who shared our beginnings. Perhaps this is why organisations like Friends Reunited became popular. Maybe, as we grow older, all the roles we've acquired in life – career woman, wife, mother, second wife, stepmum, granny, boss – will mean less than they did, and we'll return to the essence of who we were before we became all those things. Maybe then it will make good sense to have friends around who understand the real us.

MAKING NEW FRIENDS

Making friends is like riding a bicycle: you never quite forget how to do it even if you're out of practice.

I only ever met one friendless person. Although I felt sorry for her, there was no getting away from the fact that she was a breathtakingly self-serving and self-interested individual. And that's why she had no friends. Of course, in order to have a friend, you have to *be* a friend. But this fact had somehow escaped her. However, the vast majority of us have the facility to make friends, and even if we've not done it recently, we can get back into the habit.

A mate of mine, who has masses of pals, has made many

Scientific reasons for keeping up your tally of friends

- Research from Adelaide in 2005 found that friends help us to live longer, and that a network of good mates is more likely than close family relationships to increase longevity.

- Professor Bengt Winblad, professor of Geriatric Medicine at Karolinska Institutet in Stockholm, discovered that older people who enjoy regular contact with a sizeable number of friends are less likely to develop dementia.

- According to a UCLA 2007 study, loneliness puts us at increased risk of getting various diseases, because lonely individuals develop a metabolism that makes them liable to inflammation. Some scientists believe that high levels of inflammatory activity contribute to heart disease, degenerative disorders in the brain and certain cancers.

- At the 2009 annual conference of the American Association for the Advancement of Science, researchers reported that lonely people generally have poorer health, exercise less and comfort-eat more than those with an effective social network. They concluded that being lonely is as harmful as being a smoker.

of them through the years by simply striking up a conversation with someone who looks like she might be nice, or jolly. She started doing this when she was a young mum who had recently moved to a new area – and as a result she built up a circle of friends among other women who also had kids and who lived nearby. She still adopts this technique, and it works brilliantly for her.

I've heard people say that it's impossible to make new friends once you're over 45. But this is total rot.

Columnist and pundit Yasmin Alibhai-Brown agrees that it's nonsense to stop making new friends just because you're past the first flush of youth. 'New friends keep you young,' she says. 'And anyway, sometimes old friends don't recognise the person you have become – and then you find that you only want to spend limited time with them, because you really have little left in common.'

Being interested

Dale Carnegie, of *How to Make Friends and Influence People* fame once said, 'You can make more friends in two months by being interested in other people than you can in two years by trying to get other people interested in you.'

So, when making new friends we need to remember to ask people about themselves.

Don't be a shrinking violet

We need to be bold too – and to chat to people in shops, at the bus stop and when walking the dog. Every day there are opportunities to make friends that we often miss. For example, most of us belong to associations – gyms, tennis clubs, local action groups, political parties, professional organisations, and so on — which we could use to develop new friendships. Think of all the people you're on nodding terms with. How many of those might turn out to be real friends if you put yourself out to talk to them?

Like many women, I belong to a number of professional associations. In my case they're usually connected with psychotherapy or journalism. A couple of years ago I realised that I rarely attended any of the events that these organisations held. In other words, I wrote a cheque at the beginning of the year for the privilege of belonging to these groups, but that's where my involvement stopped.

So, I decided that I would go to at least one event per year per organisation. And it's been brilliant. For a start I feel more involved with the group, but I've also made three new — and good — friends.

Do your own thing

Another great way to enlarge your social network is by pursuing leisure interests that you really like. That way, you'll have a great chance to meet other women who share your passions. Plenty of people have found that when they finally indulged their desire to do a spot of creative writing, or to go on an archaeological dig, learn how to paint or take up dancing, their social circles enlarged along with their knowledge.

Let it grow

But — optimists though most of us are — perhaps we shouldn't overload our expectations. Miracles won't happen overnight. Sometimes people fail to pursue promising friendships because they don't instantly feel as comfortable with a new person as they did with, say, a best friend who's recently gone to live in Spain.

Friendship can take a while to develop. Anyway, there are different levels of intimacy. You might find that a new friend is the perfect companion for visits to the cinema – even if you don't want to entrust your deepest secrets to him or her. There's no harm in having different friends for different activities.

Some good ways to make friends

- **Get involved in local politics**. You can do this through your MP, city/town council or parish council, or by joining action groups locally. Your local paper will be a good source of ideas and you can always google 'Getting involved in politics' and then follow links that would interest you.

- **Volunteer/charity work**. Google is a marvellous source of information, or just pick a charity that you admire and ring them up direct. You might want to look back at what I wrote on volunteering in Chapter 2.

- **Walking**. There are plenty of groups you can join, including Ramblers (formerly the Ramblers' Association).

- **Classes** in French, dancing, art, cookery, writing . . . See your local library noticeboard or contact your city/town council for further information.

- **The gym**. Try out several before you part with a

---

membership fee. You want to be sure that you will be surrounded by people you like – and who could become your friends.

- **Join a choir**. Local churches are an obvious starting point. But for a wider source of information go to the Classic FM website and type 'Why Not Join a Choir?' into their search box. Singing is a joyous thing to do and it gets oxygen racing around your body and brain. You'll almost certainly make new friends too.

- **Book groups**. Ask if your local bookshop already runs one. If not, why not set up your own? There's helpful information on how to do it on a website called Bookgroup Info.

THE WONDERS OF THE INTERNET

If you haven't yet got your head around using the Internet and email, it's time you did. We don't want any wimpish protestations here that the technology is too complex! Email is the easiest way to be in touch with pals – no matter where in the world they live. And if you've got the brain to read and engage with this book, getting yourself online should be child's play.

You can also use the Internet for finding old friends or making new ones. Try these networking websites:

- Boomer Café
- Eons
- 50 Connect

- Friends Reunited
- Sagazone

Or just type in a long-lost friend's name on Google. It's amazing who you can find that way. I found a school friend who'd moved to Scotland and become a composer! Just one word of warning: top psychologist Aric Sigman believes that if we restrict our social contact to the Internet, we may reduce levels of bonding hormones that keep us healthy. He says that these hormones are only activated when we meet friends face-to-face. So, we need a balance between real and cyber contact.

Is this what friends are for?

Woman's Hour broadcaster Jenni Murray and her two friends Jane Wilton and Sally Feldman have plans to aid each other's suicide if they ever get infirm and a burden on their families.

WHERE TO FIND OUT MORE

Bookgroup info: www.bookgroup.info
Boomer Café: www.boomercafe.com
Classic FM: www.classicfm.co.uk
Eons: www.eons.com
50 Connect: www.50connect.co.uk
Friends Reunited: www.friendsreunited.co.uk

Ramblers: www.ramblers.org.uk; tel. 020 7339 8500
Sagazone: www.sagazone.co.uk

YOU WON'T STRIKE GOLD EVERY TIME

During my newfound enthusiasm for maximising my opportunities to make friends, I trotted along to a social event during a psychotherapy conference. And I tried hard to speak to new people, rather than stay in my comfort zone and talk only to those individuals I already knew. One woman seemed sassy and fun. She had an intelligent face and a wry smile – and a witty line in sarcasm.

Over a glass or two of red wine we got on like a house on fire. So, I emailed her after the conference and suggested we meet for lunch. Oh God. Was I ever wrong about anyone?

In the sober light of day, her sarcasm no longer struck me as witty but mean-minded. She droned on about all the people she was jealous of. And one by one, she rubbished a lot of colleagues I know – and like. Actually, she never shut up. She even spoke while she was eating – oblivious to the fact that morsels of food continually dropped from her mouth. I couldn't wait for the lunch to end.

When it finally did, she said, 'We must do this again.'

Over my dead body, I thought. You win some, you lose some . . .

CHAPTER 11

No Place Like Home

'There is nothing like staying at home for real comfort.'
(Jane Austen)

Our living arrangements have been very different from those of our mothers. Unlike them, we didn't tend to stay at home until we got married. Also, lots of us have lived in flat shares. Many of us have had several live-in partners, so have changed our domestic situations more often than women in previous generations. Loads of us have owned our own homes, and some of us have even lived in squats or hippie communes.

So, it stands to reason that we won't want to spend our last years in the same ways as our mothers and grand-mothers did. Most particularly, what we collectively want to avoid is going into a care home. In fact, in my own survey, 95 per cent of female baby boomers were opposed to this option. We're determined not to end our days sitting in our own poo and pee in some impersonal place where no one has a clue who we really are – and where we're force-fed TV programmes we'd never choose for ourselves.

So where do we want to live as we grow older? Well, a massive 76 per cent of us want to stay in our own homes – preferably forever.

LOCATION, LOCATION, LOCATION

But are we already living in that home? Not all of us. Plenty of boomers have unfulfilled dreams of moving somewhere different. And for many of us the question of location is much more important than the type of property we inhabit.

We're not keen on traditional 'retirement' venues – like Torquay, Bournemouth and Eastbourne – but a sizeable minority of women who answered my questionnaire did say that they longed to live by the sea. However, in the main they favour resorts with a city feel, like Brighton, rather than the sleepy coastal towns and villages our grand-parents used to move to.

Professor Richard Webber of King's College London told me that we baby boomers are much more individu-alistic than our parents and grandparents were. He says that in the past, people were happy to move somewhere known to be a favourite retirement haunt, because they felt they'd have guaranteed things in common with other inhabitants. We're not like that at all.

When I was small, my paternal grandfather retired from his job as a subpostmaster and he and my grandmother moved to a village on the south coast of England where neither of them knew anybody. He was fine. As an energetic, confident man he threw himself into gardening – and winning prizes at horticulture shows – watching cricket and walking along the coast. He didn't make friends. But then he never had. I don't think any of us gave much thought to my poor grandmother. Once they had moved, she certainly never made any new friends and spent her time cleaning the house, reading and watching television. The only possible source of pals might have been the local church, which they both attended, but none of those parishioners ever came to their home as far as I remember. Not surprisingly, my granny aged quickly.

Maybe you've witnessed similar situations in your own family. Is this what we want for ourselves? Definitely not!

Second homes and relocating

Of course, unlike previous generations, some boomers have second homes, which they plan to turn into their sole home one day. The great thing is that by the time that day comes they're already involved with the community and have lots of contacts and friends. That gradual transition is a totally different experience from uprooting and going somewhere they've never lived before.

A growing trend, which was highlighted in a survey conducted by Experian, is for people of our age – particularly those running their own businesses – to relocate to market towns such as Aberfeldy, Aylsham, Beverley, Buxton, Hexham, Ludlow, Ruthin, Stamford, Thame, Totnes and Woodbridge.

Another option for us – which is not a choice that our mums or grandmothers would have been likely to make –

is to live in a city centre. I know lots of women who are doing this – or planning to. They can walk to the doctor, the dentist, the shops and the library – or take the bus. They enrol on arts courses or involve themselves in politics. They get discounts at cinemas or theatres. They thrill to the atmosphere of street markets, and value the contrasting quietness of parks and squares; and they generally enjoy the diversity and the stimulation on offer. I think this is a great choice for us. If we're surrounded by masses of stuff going on, this will keep us young. And in terms of mental health it's much better for us than being isolated and dependent on a car to get around – because one day that vehicle may be too expensive to run, or we may reach an age where we no longer feel confident about driving.

Other female baby boomers are currently hedging their bets – being not sure as yet whether they'll end up as town or country people – and have downsized from a large family home into two smaller dwellings. Typically one of their places is in a village and the other is city based.

A move in the right direction

Whatever your inclination, any move you make in the next few years could be your last, and it will define the kind of older age that you have. So, it's vital to get it right.

For some of us the challenges have got greater since the recession, because our savings or properties are not worth what they were before, and we're concerned that our money may not stretch to do what we want.

Another point to remember is that if we're not going to conventionally 'retire' – and most of us are not – we need to be where we can continue to study, or run our own businesses, or do part-time jobs. And if we want our home to help pay for itself – by renting out part of it to other people – we have to think about where it would be easier to do that. A university town or city would obviously provide a likelier source of income than a rural hamlet.

If you're undecided about where you want to be, try making a list of your important requirements. You might feel, for example, that you must:

- Live in a town
- Be near a train station
- Have a theatre in the vicinity
- Be within walking distance of a doctor, shops, library, cinema and swimming pool
- Be within an hour of children/grandchildren
- Be near some existing friends

Listing your priorities should help you see the future more clearly.

LIVING ABROAD

But what if you've always longed to move abroad? In some ways, this is easier than it's ever been, because pension arrangements are more flexible than they used to be. Masses of people follow this particular dream, and never look back. I can think of several who seem really happy, including two 50-something women running a gorgeous bed-and-breakfast place in a French rural paradise. And you probably know friends or colleagues who've moved to another country, and who love it and would never return.

In the last few years, however, many such dreams have turned to nightmares – and the worldwide recession has altered many people's perceptions of what they can afford, or what they want. So, if you're thinking of living in foreign parts, do read the following comments from women who did it, but who now regret that decision.

My husband was made redundant. We'd always longed to live in the sun, so we booked ourselves on one of those Inspection Tours in Spain. They told us how great the weather was, how cheap it was and what a wonderful lifestyle we'd have. So when we were offered a sizeable discount to buy an apartment off-plan, we jumped at it. When we moved, initially it seemed like an extended holiday. Later, we discovered that it's not sunny 52 weeks a year. February can be really cold and the houses are often like ice boxes. Also, in the summer, it gets so hot we couldn't go anywhere or do anything. It was awful.

Medical care is excellent in much of Europe, but when I got ill unexpectedly, though I was impressed with my treatment, I found it frightening to feel so poorly when everyone around me was speaking a language I couldn't understand.

I left the UK when I was 50 and hadn't paid enough National Insurance stamps to qualify for a full pension. I didn't think it would matter, as it was cheaper to live in Portugal than at home. But now it isn't. I want to go back, but I can't sell my apartment. I'm worried that even when I do return, my money won't buy much in England, and also that my pension won't be sufficient to live on. And I may not be able to get a job.

When we moved to Prague, I loved it. But my daughter in Britain has had two babies since then. And I hadn't anticipated how much I would mind that they're growing up in a different country from me.

My husband died unexpectedly. As soon as that happened, I wanted to come home. But I have no house to return to, because the one we shared before moving abroad was sold to fund our new life in Europe. I feel rootless as well as grief-stricken about him.

My partner has a chronic condition and is becoming increasingly frail. His medical care in France is better than anything we could expect on the NHS in Britain, but despite that — and the fact that we've had a home here for years and both speak the language — we want to be back in Scotland. Illness makes you long to have your family around you.

So, what do you feel about all of that? Do you still want to go? If so — good for you! But here is a list of things you might want to consider — based on what I've learned from these disenchanted expats:

1 If at all possible, keep a home back in the UK — even a shoe-box-sized flat, or something you co-own with a family member.
2 Take financial advice about foreign exchange rates.
3 Learn at least some of the language of the country you want to go to.
4 When you've decided on the area you think you want to live in, rent a property for at least six months — preferably a year — before purchasing anything.

5 When you do buy, don't get something in a block where everyone else is British. You didn't come abroad to live in a UK commune, and these properties can be hard to sell if you want to leave. Instead, get somewhere you can integrate properly with local people.

6 Before even thinking about moving abroad, contact HM Revenue & Customs. There's lots of information about tax and pensions on their website.

CHOOSING THE HOUSING THAT'S RIGHT FOR YOU

Once you've thought about location – whether it's at home or abroad – you can then start to think about what type of housing is going to suit you for the next 30 years. I said at the beginning of this chapter that the vast majority of us want to stay in our homes. But Gillian Connor, who is Age Concern's very knowledgeable housing expert, said that we may need to re-think what we mean by our 'own home'. She says that many of our current homes will be too expensive for us long term, and also that they may be impractical if we become less mobile.

Gillian told me that when politicians talk about 'independent living', they don't really mean what we mean by being in our 'own home'. Their meaning is simply 'not a care home' but somewhere we own or rent where we have 'security of tenure'.

It seems early for people who are as young and vital as

we are to have to think about where we're going to end up, but the more I look into the whole housing thing, the more I realise that we need to get our heads around what the possibilities are, so that we don't find events overtaking us, leaving us only with the options we'd hate.

So, here are some different types of housing we may want to consider.

Extra care

The term 'extra care' means housing for older people where care services are provided. One such 'extra care option' would be a small complex of perhaps 30 to 40 homes. This is really what we know as 'sheltered housing'.

There are many variations in what might be provided, but the crucial element is that there must be a 24-hour care team. The idea is that individuals could live in such a place for a long time, with help from the support team, and sustained by the company of other similar residents.

To me, this sounds pretty grim and far too 'old' for us!

The other current 'extra care' plan is for retirement villages – which you may have seen advertised in the property pages of the posh papers. In each village there is a minimum of one hundred homes: this scale of development allows for a greater range of care services and facilities on-site than would be viable if the settlement were smaller.

Some of the big players in this concept are The Joseph Rowntree Foundation, The Extra Care Charitable Trust, the Anchor Trust, Audley Retirement and Richmond Villages. There are a variety of housing options within these villages, including owner-occupied, rental and shared ownership.

I've been told that these developments evoke an excellent 'residents' culture'. They also feel safe. And couples find it reassuring that they'll probably be able to remain in the village, even if one of them becomes less well or mobile, and that the longer-lived partner can stay in their home after the death of their spouse.

The villages typically have a hairdresser, restaurant, coffee shop, Internet/computer room, music room and a shop, as well as a leisure centre and pool. And of course there's a 24-hour on-site care and support team.

But the thing is that these 'extra care' schemes are supposed to appeal to us while we're still relatively fit and able – as early as 60. And I'm not at all sure that they will cut the mustard with us.

Quite apart from anything else, a lot of this sort of housing is small, or has small rooms. So, where are we going to entertain? Where will our grandchildren stay when they want to visit? Where will our stuff go?

I remember seeing tears in the eyes of a retiring and normally unemotional Scottish doctor at the thought of having to abandon most of his books when he and his wife moved into a retirement bungalow.

Well, with us it's not just books: there's the music system, the CD and record collections, the computer and printer, maybe a guitar or drum kit – and a lifetime's collection of paraphernalia that we couldn't possibly do without.

Cohousing projects

Another option is something called cohousing. The UK Cohousing Network describes this as: 'a way of living, which brings individuals and families together in groups to share common aims and activities – while also enjoying their own self-contained accommodation and personal space.'

Wikipedia defines it in this way: 'A cohousing community is a kind of intentional community composed of private homes with full kitchens, supplemented by extensive common facilities.'

One thing that immediately appeals to me about this is that it's not an older person's ghetto. It's for all ages who want to live in this kind of way. You can read up about various initiatives on the Cohousing Network website.

I'm pretty sure that cohousing will suit many boomers. It feels quite jolly and stimulating and independent. I also suspect it will be a good option for gay women. There are far more women 'out' as lesbians in our generation than in previous ones, and as most of them don't have children – and may be without a partner – cohousing could well appeal to them.

Cohousing is far more advanced in various European countries, including Holland and Denmark, than it is here – but it's catching on the UK. And it does occur to me that if we want to live with our friends around us, there may be scope for several of us to buy – or rent – within the same cohousing project.

Homeshare

Many of us will probably consider the idea of having lodgers when we get older as a way of staying in our own houses. In fact, plenty of divorced female baby boomers who have retained the marital home already let out rooms to young professionals or students in order to make ends meet financially. However, there may come a time when we're less able to cope with finding tenants or keeping on top of all the chores that having them entails. So a next logical step would be to opt for a system called Homeshare.

Homeshare is an organised arrangement where a householder – who is willing to share her home and who may be at a stage in life where she needs some support – is matched with an individual who needs accommodation, and is willing to offer help to the householder in exchange for somewhere to stay.

This scheme could have tremendous appeal for older people who have a home they don't want to leave, but who are beginning to feel too vulnerable to live alone. You can get more information from Homeshare International.

Currently, the scheme operates in various countries including Australia, Austria, Canada, Germany, New Zealand, Spain, the UK and the US.

Living with friends

Many of us are planning to live with friends – particularly if we outlive our partners. And in my survey, several baby boomers described how this might work:

> *I'd like a courtyard with half a dozen chums all living in their own places round it.*

> *My aim is to buy a large house with five of my girlfriends. In that way we can have a nice life, and hopefully we'll have enough money left over from selling our own properties to pay for a nurse or other help if one of us needs it.*

Great idea, count me in. But I'm not living with that Angela... or Maureen... or Rowena... or Susan. And don't even MENTION Melanie.

Sounds great! And it makes sense to consider pooling resources — especially in these financially uncertain times.

Until recently, the trend has been for more and more people to opt for single living in search of having 'our own space'. But it looks like the economic downturn may halt this fashion. Another reason for not living alone — as we've already seen in this book — is that experts believe it's far harder to stay mentally healthy if you're isolated in old age.

So, for health reasons, as well as financial ones, there's much to be said for sharing our homes with friends as we get older. But it will take planning.

When are we going to discuss it? When will we think the time is right to move in with our mates? And have we thought of the legal implications? It would be awful if we always meant to get round to it, but never quite sorted it until we were too old or knocked off to do it.

One major worry, of course, is how to sort out 'house-rules'. Suppose one of your friends has a feckless son who sponges off her and — given half a chance — might come and stay for months on end? Somehow you'd need to think of these things before moving in. Not easy.

Making proper arrangements

Yasmin Rumjahn, who is a conveyancing solicitor, warned me that lawyers would treat a transaction where friends plan to live together with 'particular concern'. She said that a solicitor would have to ensure that there is no 'coercion or undue influence' implied in the arrangement, and that the client 'fully understood the implications of entering into such a transaction'. She added that the 'repercussions

of a "friendly agreement" going sour could be very traumatic, so arrangements in writing (agreed and signed by
all parties) would need to be in place to avoid unneces-
sary distress and dispute.' She also said that there would
be a host of legal issues to be sorted.

One big stumbling block would be if the women
concerned had children they wanted to leave money to.
Of course many of us don't have offspring, which would
make life simpler. But in all shared households, there would
have to be agreements about what would happen if someone
died, or got too infirm to continue with the arrangement,
or wanted out and therefore wished to force a sale.

Yasmin suggested that the best way forward would be
to hold the property in trust – which would require a
Declaration of Trust agreement to be drawn up. She also
said that you'd need to ensure that all parties had independent legal advice about inheritance issues.

So, basically, everyone concerned would need their own
solicitor to advise on personal matters, and there would
also need to be a conveyancing solicitor for buying the
property, and a more specialist lawyer for drawing up a
trust.

A new way?

All the above sounds complicated doesn't it? But I don't
think it should put us off. When we were young, we were
often told that we couldn't do things – or that people like
us couldn't expect to achieve the ambitions we held dear
– but we went ahead anyway, and changed the world. So,
if sufficient numbers of us decide that we want to live with

our friends, my bet is that solicitors will start specialising in this particular area. But we do need to realise that there are legal complexities to be sorted out, and if we're serious about living with our mates later on, we probably need to start planning for it sooner rather than later.

Interestingly, a young colleague told me that in Switzerland 'house-sharing amongst women of age 60 and upwards is becoming more and more popular, as it prevents them from becoming lonely and, because everyone is looking after each other, it delays the time when they may have to consider going into an old people's home.' So, it's not just us Brits who are blazing a trail with new ideas of how we'll live over the next few decades.

Multi-generational living

Perhaps you've been thinking that it might be socially and financially helpful to live with some of your family. I've noticed that one of the side effects of the recession is that many people are becoming much more family minded. Tough times tend to focus our minds on what we think is really important in life – and for many of us that includes our families.

It's a small step from thinking how much you'd like to see more of your children and grandchildren to wondering if you could live with them. And lots of us are beginning to think this way – so much so that there is a name for it, which is multi-generational living. The idea is that two generations both sell their respective homes and pool their resources so that they can afford a large and suitable property for them all to live together.

According to a study carried out by the Prudential in 2008, more than 80,000 people in the UK are living in homes which house at least three generations of the same family. The Pru expects this number to increase.

Rupert Fisher of Savills Estate Agency says that in rural areas – such as Lincolnshire where he is based – there are many former farms and other large properties that are ideal for extended-family living.

It's easy to see the benefits. A youngish couple who don't have the means to buy a big family house are able to live in a much larger property than they could normally afford. The parents/grandparents get to live in close proximity to family within the large property, but retain their privacy by having their own accommodation including, ideally, a separate front door, bathroom and kitchen.

Everyone then benefits from helping each other in the form of shopping, assistance with difficult paperwork, babysitting or whatever. Also, the children in the house have constant access to grandparents and can enjoy what is often a very special relationship.

A permanent guest

If you have no family – or don't get on with them – you may perhaps have wondered about living in a hotel. I've always thought that I'd love to do this if I'm on my own in my dotage. But perhaps I've read too many Somerset Maugham short stories, where dotty old dames live out their last years in formerly grand hotels on Lake Geneva!

It seems like a great option. People cook for you and clean your room. There are tourists to talk to in the dining room. You don't need to find money for the gas or electricity or water bills, and there's no council tax. All you have to do is negotiate a long-term deal with the hotel and pay that bill. Perfect!

So, I thought I'd find out how easy it would be.

Much to my amazement, no hotel owner I spoke to was at all enthusiastic about the idea. A charming young man at a particularly lovely hotel where we recently stayed in south-west Ireland put a right damper on it.

'Oooh, I don't think we'd want anyone here long term,' he said. 'They would probably start expecting special treatment and wouldn't fit in with the rest of the guests.'

'But,' I said, 'what about the fact that you'd have my money as a regular contribution you could depend on?'

'Oh no,' he said. 'You'd be wanting cut-price deals and we'd probably not do as well out of you as we do out of the other visitors. And you'd be wanting your own things around you . . . oh I don't think so.'

I was crushed!

A friend of mine, Sue Paskins, who used to own and run two of the nicest hotels in Brighton, was equally unenthusiastic. She said:

Most hoteliers would not want long-term guests unless there were a number of them. They have different needs from short-term ones. Clothes space would need to be much bigger for a start. And most hotel rooms are only geared to having guests for two or three nights, which means that many of them only have showers — not baths. A long-term guest would expect both.

Also, how would they handle their washing? Would they pay over the odds for the hotel to do it, or carry to a launderette?

If they did that, there would then be the problem of ironing/airing. I can see many difficulties.

Hmm. I wasn't expecting that hotel living would be so problematic. So maybe I'll have to think again.

Now, here's a good idea!

When the *QE2* liner was retired in the summer of 2008, a curious story emerged. It turned out that Beatrice Muller, whose husband had died on a cruise some seven years earlier, had been living on the ship ever since. She had occupied a cabin costing her £3,500 per month, and she reckoned that this was no more expensive than a Florida retirement home – and much more fun!

I guess that most of us don't feel ready to make really long-term plans about where or how we'll live in the future. But even so, I believe it's time for us to bone up on the options, and also to be aware of possible problems concerning some of our – as yet – sketchy plans.

We can't know for sure at this stage how well we'll be in 15 years, or whether or not we'll outlive our partners, or indeed what will happen to the world's economy. But I think that if we're serious in our determination to avoid the dreaded care home, we need to start pondering how best to do that.

WHERE TO FIND OUT MORE

Age Concern: www.ageconcern.org.uk; tel. 0800 009966

Anchor Trust: www.anchor.org.uk

Audley: www.audleyretirement.co.uk

Cohousing: www.cohousing.org.uk

Extra Care Charitable Trust: http://extracare.hcldev.co.uk

HM Revenue & Customs: www.hmrc.gov.uk; tel. 0191 203 7010 (for people living and working abroad)

Homeshare: www.naaps.org.uk/en/homeshare

Homeshare International: http://homeshare.org

Joseph Rowntree Housing Trust: www.jrht.org.uk

Richmond Villages: www.richmond-villages.com/

Savills Estate Agents: www.savills.co.uk

CHAPTER 12

The Time of Our Lives

'The best of times is now.' (La Cage aux Folles)

I was in a café the other day when I overheard this conversation:

'I do belly dancing on Monday, French on a Tuesday, and go to the Spirtualist church on Fridays and Sundays,' said one woman.

'And I do creative writing on a Wednesday and Pilates on Saturday. So, if we're going to do that salsa class it'll have to be on Thursday,' replied her friend.

Of course, they were baby boomers. How different we are in mid life compared with our mothers. We're having the best of times!

THE BOOMER ZEST FOR LIFE

In fact, when I assessed my survey results, I was amazed at all the activities we get up to – and also at our plans for the future, which include:

- Building an eco house
- Living on a boat
- Writing an opera
- Buying a Harley Davidson motorbike
- Visiting all the cathedrals in England
- Finding the perfect shade of blonde hair dye
- Learning flamenco dancing

But our top 20 ambitions are:

1 Travelling – for example, the great rail journeys of the world, backpacking around China, or walking the Inca trail
2 Being happy
3 Spending more time with the family – particularly grandchildren
4 Getting/staying fit and active
5 Being healthy
6 Having more contact with friends
7 Writing a book
8 Being financially secure
9 Achieving a better work–life balance
10 Continuing to be happy with our current romantic partner
11 Continuing to work

12 Getting more education – everything from
   A levels to a PhD
13 Going to concerts, galleries, operas, ballets, exhibitions and plays
14 Developing a business or creative project
15 Volunteering – at home or abroad
16 Finding a new relationship
17 Living abroad – at least some of the time
18 Learning a new language
19 Learning a musical instrument
20 Doing more singing/joining a choir

What writing this book has also taught me is that female
baby boomers elsewhere in the world are just like us. Claire,
who is French but who lives in England, says:

> *Quite a few French women I know have started, or are thinking
> of starting, new projects post 40 and even post 50. Among my
> acquaintances, many middle-class women are looking forward to
> early retirement – particularly if they have been* fonctionnaires
> *[civil servants]. This enables them to devote time to new things;
> not necessarily full-blown new careers, but certainly fulfilling –
> and sometimes lucrative – activities.*

Australian psychologist Robyn Vickers-Willis, author of
Navigating Midlife: Women Becoming Themselves, reckons that
there's masses of common ground between UK boomers
and those 'down-under'. She said:

> *Many of us are living our lives very differently from our
> mother's generation – for obvious reasons of financial inde-
> pendence/divorce/increased opportunities – and are exploring*

a variety of interests through adult education or workshops. I believe that all this is contributing to more women navigating a mid-life transition: a time when our psyche is encouraging us to break away from our conditioning, and create a life based on a greater understanding of who we truly are.

And a Swiss friend told me:

In Switzerland, women past 45 become much more active and tackle new challenges with ambition and optimism. Their kids have left the house and they can do something for themselves, for a change. Many get into sport. They also join societies and clubs to meet others with similar interests, and many go back into education. They also go travelling.

BECOMING EXPLORERS

Travelling clearly appeals to female baby boomers wherever in the world they live. Many of us want to travel with our partners – perhaps by buying an old camper van and pootling through Europe.

We're also increasingly keen on railways, because they're less environmentally damaging – and much less of a palaver – than flying. If you haven't already found it, check out a wonderful website – The Man in Seat Sixty-One – which can help you plan railway journeys worldwide.

Unfortunately, many female baby boomers have partners who don't share their enthusiasm for globetrotting. And of course plenty of us don't actually have partners. So we're looking to travel with other women. And if we don't have friends who are keen to accompany us, we're signing up with organisations that bring female voyagers together.

One such group is Women Traveling Together. Their spokeswoman told me that there's a general perception that 'travelling' must mean going off on safari or back-packing in Peru. But she said that lots of women just want to go to mainstream destinations like Paris, Venice or Vienna.

The great thing about Women Traveling Together is that it doesn't matter where you're starting from, as the trips don't include travel from the home country. You just meet at the destination.

Another way of seeing the world is through volunteering. If you're interested in doing that, contact either VSO or Gap Year for Grown Ups. There are more details on both of them in Chapter 2.

STILL TIME . . .

Travel is just part of our future picture. We're also taking up fresh challenges at home. After all, there's still time for us to learn new things, and to make a difference to our own lives and those of other people.

Politics could be a way of doing that. Following the MPs' expenses scandal of 2009, many of us feel so aggrieved about sleazy politicians that we've vowed to get involved ourselves. Lynn Faulds Wood – baby boomer, long-time campaigner and former *Watchdog* presenter – is planning to stand as an independent candidate at the next general election. And so is TV presenter Esther Rantzen.

The rest of us may not have the public profile to get into parliament, but we could become involved in local campaigns that we feel passionate about, or put ourselves up for the local parish or town council. Loads of us were very politically motivated when we were young, so maybe it would feel good to get involved again now.

The courage to try something new

If not politics, there are plenty of other challenges. Naturally, we sometimes feel diffident and wonder if we really can master something new; for example, plenty of women who are now taking degrees have had to struggle with worries that their memory might not be up to absorbing lots of new facts. And women planning to start businesses are frequently anxious that they might be viewed as stupid or naive. It's sad how our old timidity can rear its head at the least convenient times!

But think what we've achieved already. It's fantastic. And even if a new challenge requires us to alter how we've always perceived ourselves, there's no reason why we shouldn't rise to the occasion.

Michael Neenan — author of *Developing Resilience: A Cognitive-Behavioural Approach* — says: 'Our beliefs and behaviours are not fixed in perpetuity. And if, for whatever reason, they have outlived their usefulness, we can develop new ones – so long as we're prepared to be curious about what changes are needed, and to develop an experimental outlook.'

Act now!

The main thing is not to procrastinate – because that may well be the thief of all our future hopes and dreams. But if we get a move on, we could even become really expert in something new. Well, we could if we had 10,000 hours to spare! You see, an eminent psychologist and academic called Dr K. Anders Ericsson made a study of professional musicians and he discovered that the real difference between orchestral players and outstanding virtuoso soloists was not musicality or talent, but practice! The virtuosos had all put in 10,000 hours or more of training – which was far more than the also-rans.

Now, I doubt if any of us are going to become virtuosos now, but if we could put aside six hours a week to practise a new skill – maybe for 48 weeks in a year – then we'd have 288 hours under our belt by the end of the first year. In five years, that would accumulate to 1,440 hours, which is more than a seventh of the way towards becoming a real expert!

Many of us know how easy it is to let years go by while we think about – rather than do – something new. So it's intriguing to realise that in the time we might put something off, we could actually become proficient at it.

What's next?

I said earlier in this chapter that many of us are keen to start new businesses. One of the most exciting projects I've encountered is a brand new network for our generation, called Next Challenges. It's the 'baby' of two highly successful business women, and will be a comprehensive website for those of us baby boomers who have always worked and had lots of stimulus in our careers, but who are now preparing to adjust to life beyond that.

I think Next Challenges will appeal to many of us who possibly don't find the current 50-plus websites particularly exciting or appropriate for us. Next Challenges will launch in early 2010. If you're interested in finding out more, email its founders, Jean Garon or Lesley Pocock.

Books for the women we are now

The View From Here by Joan Bakewell
Over the Hill and Between the Sheets by Gail Belsky
The Year of Magical Thinking by Joan Didion
Reading in Bed by Sue Gee
Eat, Pray, Love by Elizabeth Gilbert
Just Me by Sheila Hancock
The Two of Us: My Life with John Thaw by Sheila Hancock
No! I Don't Want to Join a Bookclub by Virginia Ironside
A Round-heeled Woman by Jane Juska
Fifty is Not a Four-Letter Word by Linda Kelsey
I Feel Bad About My Neck by Nora Ephron

ADJUSTING TO MID-LIFE CHANGES

One of the reasons for launching Next Challenges is that so many of us baby boomers have worked throughout our lives and are likely to feel rather lost when we stop.

Retirement takes some adjusting to, and even if we have plans to start a business or volunteer, or see more of friends, or travel, we may still struggle to find relevance and structure in our lives.

Professor Jan Pahl says that retirement is particularly difficult for individuals who have really enjoyed work, or identified themselves through it. She says men often found this tough, but that now it's just as likely for career women to feel utterly bereft when they have to move on.

We can feel lost

On a basic level, it's sometimes quite difficult to know what to wear! If your wardrobe is stuffed full of business suits, it can be a challenge to decide how you want to look once all that formal gear is no longer appropriate. As a recently retired client of mine said: 'I bought some lovely "smart casual" clothes from the Boden catalogue, but I don't feel like me when I wear them.'

So, leaving work can leave us with a sense of loss. And there could be other losses too:

- We may feel we've lost our role when our kids leave home.
- We may grieve about our youthful looks disappearing when we see our mother spookily staring at us out of the mirror.
- We might also feel grief-stricken when friends die, or if they become unavailable to us through dementia.
- And there's no doubt that many of us dread the

loss of a partner. A substantial number of women in my survey put it as their 'greatest fear'.

Losing the one we love

I know that if my husband dies before me, I will feel extremely lost and miserable. But it's not something that is easy to prepare for.

Some feisty women who are older than us – notably novelist Joan Didion and actress Sheila Hancock – have already had to deal with losing hugely loved partners, and what emerges from their writing is that they hadn't anticipated how alien the world would seem, and how devastated they would feel as widows – especially since they had always seen themselves as eminently capable people.

So, grief may hit us hard. But we need to accept that there is no shame in going to pieces when someone close dies. In fact, it's normal. We're supposed to feel unutterably sad when a huge part of our life ends. But that won't make it easier to bear.

If or when it happens – even though we've been such independent women – we should allow our friends and family to look after and comfort us. And even if we've never needed counselling before, it's useful to know that there are private bereavement therapists in most countries, and that in the UK we also have a voluntary organisation called Cruse, whose counsellors are expert in supporting individuals as they grieve over someone's death.

Our spiritual selves

I believe it will be helpful too if we find an element of spirituality – or even just some acceptance of life's cycles – that may have been lacking in our lives until now. Many baby boomers were brought up to go to church, but vast numbers of us abandoned organised religion a long time ago. And even if we didn't, we may feel ill-equipped to deal with the events that the next decades may throw at us.

I think it would help to take a leaf out of the Stoic philosophers' book. They believed that we should view our lives – and the good things in them – as temporary gifts, rather than as our right.

In recent decades it's been common for people in developed countries to expect things to go brilliantly – which may be one reason why we're so amazed when banks crash, or terrorists strike, or floods wipe out whole communities. But life is full of reverses – even if we haven't had many so far. And there may be more as we get older. We may, for instance, find that our memories, or our bodies, become less reliable. And, as a result, we may be very self-critical. But the truth is that we will be doing our best with whatever faculties we have at that stage of our lives. So, although we've been an impatient generation, it would be wise to learn to be more patient with ourselves.

There is no shame in being older. It happens to everyone who's lucky enough to live long enough. But it is a time for being compassionate to ourselves rather than critical. This doesn't mean that we have to be indulgent – or to stop eating healthily and exercising and keeping our brains alert – but it does mean that we should be accepting and kind to ourselves when inevitable changes occur.

Mindfulness

You may have heard of 'mindfulness' – particularly if you know anything about Buddhism. The dictionary defines it as 'taking thought or care of'. But in recent years, it has grown into a technique used by psychologists and psychotherapists to help their clients get into a state of mind in which they can truly live and focus in 'the moment'.

Often when we are mentally distressed or physically ill, we make things worse by trying our hardest to flee from the feelings that we have. But mindfulness helps us to feel calmly aware of things as they really are and to focus on what is actually going on in any given moment, rather than what we wish to be happening.

Mindfulness is becoming increasingly useful in the treatment of anxiety and depression. And I'm sure it could be a useful tool for us if we're looking to deal with our losses or our frailties in a more accepting way.

One way of becoming 'mindful' is simply to sit quietly, breathing deeply, and focusing on one part of the body, such as the tip of the nose. You might find it helpful to breathe in for a count of three, and to breathe out to a count of four. This seems to help generate a mood of calm and tranquillity.

Another very good 'mindful' exercise is to spend 10 minutes contemplating a raisin. I have to tell you that when I first saw this technique done on a training video, I thought it was totally barmy! However, not long afterwards, I had a patient who was extremely distressed and agitated. As chance would have it, I'd bought myself a bag of nuts and dried fruit for lunch, so I decided to try the raisin technique.

It had a profoundly quietening and peaceful effect on her. And I was so impressed that I've used it with lots of other patients since.

The raisin technique

1 Take a raisin and hold it in one hand, then focus on it as if you've never seen one before. Look at it searchingly. Notice how many grooves there are in it. How many little raised bobbles. Whether the colour is the same throughout. Whether it's symmetrical or misshapen. Use your eyes to really see it in a very intent and exploring way.

2 After a minute or so, alter your focus to the feel of it. You might want to close your eyes. Does it feel smooth? Soft? Sticky? Rough where the grooves are? Roll it between your middle finger and your thumb. Focus on its touch.

3 Now lift the raisin to your nose. Can you get any scent from it? Breathe in slowly and notice any aroma.

4 Next, gently place your raisin in your mouth. Just let it lie on your tongue for a while. Then move it around inside your mouth. Gently play with it.

5 Eventually, press your teeth on to it without biting through it. What do you notice? A change of smell? A

sweet taste? Focus on the experience and how intense the flavour is. Then, gently bite right through it – and notice how the taste increases and lingers on your tongue. When you are ready, swallow it.

6 Sit awhile, noticing the feeling as the raisin begins its journey down to your stomach. Notice the taste and smell that remains in your mouth and the slight stick-iness on your fingers.

7 Breathe in and out slowly. And just be.

The above exercise is very peaceful to carry out. And it could be a useful technique for you to do every day – or at least whenever you feel in pain, or stressed or angry. It is a form of meditation that soothes the brain.

There are plenty of other mindfulness techniques. And if you google 'mindfulness' you can even watch small video demonstrations. There are also plenty of books on the subject.

Of course you may already be into meditation, yoga or self-hypnosis. Or you may get all the soul feeding you need from being a practising Buddhist, Christian, Hindu, Jew, Moslem or Sikh. We all have to find what works for us.

GETTING ORGANISED

Another thing that I have vowed to attend to before too much longer is just getting organised. Having cleared out my parents' home after their deaths, I have promised myself that I will simplify my affairs as I get older, and not leave utter chaos for someone else to plough through.

You may have similar plans, but it's hard to know just when to start clearing up. Obviously, if you are planning to move, that's your ideal opportunity. Even then, there may be things you want to keep for a while longer – but don't want others to find if you pop your clogs.

I have a friend who had a long-term and beautiful affair. She has kept all the letters she received from her lover during that period, and is most reluctant to part with them. The trouble is that during the affair she was married to someone else. And her children have no knowledge that she was unfaithful to their father – and she would prefer to keep it that way.

She is a vital and energetic baby boomer – and may well live to 100! But she knows that there are no guarantees, and that she ought to find a safe place for those letters soon. Many of us have treasures that are so personal we'd sooner our relatives knew nothing about them, so perhaps we should ask friends to keep them for us. Just a thought . . .

Making final arrangements

Another task we may yet need to tackle is making a will – which I talked about in Chapter 3. Also, many of us want to put in place some strategies for a future when we are too infirm to manage our own affairs; for example, we may want to complete and register a lasting power of attorney in which a relative or friend is nominated to make decisions for us if we're no longer able to take them.

We might also want to make a Living Will (this is now often called an Advance Decision, or Advance Directive), so that we can clarify which medical treatments we would like – or not like – to receive, should we lose mental capacity in the future. There's lots of information about this on the Direct Gov website in the Government, Citizens and Rights section. Or you can get advice and the appropriate documents from Law Pack.

We possibly might also want to make our views known on assisted suicide. While I was writing this chapter, the conductor Sir Edward Downes and his wife went to Dignitas to end their lives. Although many people think this was wrong, I personally feel that it was brave, touching and dignified. Of course, I don't know at this stage how I would react if I became terminally ill. But I suspect that I wouldn't want to struggle on beyond the point where my life feels valuable – and I would certainly prefer to be able to leave any money I have to my niece, nephew and step-grandchildren, rather than use it to bolster the profits of some nursing home. That's my choice. You may want to think about yours.

A SIMPLER LIFE

Hopefully, we still have plenty of viable time left and we may want to use it to do simpler and more creative things than we have in the past; for example, by learning various useful crafts.

These days there are a myriad of websites and organisations to help:

- The Make Lounge runs workshops that teach you how to 'make do and mend' in a fashionable way.
- The Internet Craft Fair has good information on creating jewellery, learning woodwork and getting into silk painting.
- The Low Impact Living Initiative website advises on all sorts of useful skills, including how to customise your wardrobe.
- And if you just fancy sewing or knitting in the company of other women, check out Stitch 'n' Bitch, and Knit and Natter.

The 'forest dweller' way

Another way to simplify life might be to become a 'forest dweller'. This idea stems from a form of Hindu teaching, in which there are various stages in life after childhood. The first part is for study, and the second for marrying and becoming householders. But in the third stage, once people's hair is grey and they've become grandparents, they can go off to live in the forest – relinquishing business affairs, home, money and control in favour of their adult children.

Although I've heard of baby boomers retreating to crofts on loch sides, or seeking solitude in cottages miles from anywhere, I doubt if many of us would be keen to disappear off and live in a real forest. But it might be appealing to create a kind of 'forest dweller' state of mind.

Perhaps we could allow ourselves time to notice the sun shining or the birds singing. We might also like the idea of living more simply – in terms of diet and clothes – and enjoying more thinking time.

I believe it's natural to want more of this kind of simple quality time as we grow older. I confess I've started thinking about how complex life is today, and about additives, chemicals and pollutants in food, air and cosmetics. It suddenly seems to me that in the past hundred years or so we've been asking far too much of our bodies, which were conditioned for millennia before that to deal with cleaner and quieter environments.

Is my current way of thinking something that happens with age? Or is it about saving the planet? Or has it something to do with the recession, which is making lots of us reappraise what is genuinely important?

Back to the earth

I'm not sure why many of us feel that way, but one thing I noticed in the results of my questionnaire was just how many baby boomers long to create gardens and grow things – much like a modern version of the old television favourite, *The Good Life*.

In fact, there's currently rather a 'blitz spirit' about 'growing your own' – not just to save money but for ecological reasons too.

In London, for example, campaigning journalist Rosie Boycott is working for Mayor Boris as London Food Champion and one of her aims is to get the rooftops of big businesses converted into market gardens.

Also, the National Trust has announced that it's going to create 1,000 allotment plots on its land to give local communities the chance to grow their own fruit and vegetables. And some of us simply want to look after our own gardens, and plant herbs and flowers — because it feels soothing, and we never had time before. Of course, older people in previous generations did that too — but we can't be different all the time!

WHAT REALLY MATTERS

I've said elsewhere in this book that the recession has made us more aware of what really matters in life. And I think that as we grow older, the people we value most will play an increasing part in our lives. Of course family members – like siblings, children and grandchildren – are very special to most of us. But what may be more surprising is how you feel drawn to your cousins as you age.

If your family is anything like mine, your cousins are spread around the country – or maybe the globe. You may have had holidays together as children and gone to each other's weddings, but often contact with them has been sporadic since then. As older relations die – parents, and aunts and uncles – family funerals crop up with increasing regularity. And these occasions give us a chance to speak to family we're closely related to, but hardly know. And in some cases, becoming close to a cousin can be hugely enjoyable.

Also, because of the Internet, lots of us are now doing our family trees – and cousins can be very useful in helping with details we never knew or have forgotten. Recently, the organisation called Find My Past put the 1911 census online. This is fantastically interesting – not least because it's the first census where the original handwriting of our relatives has been preserved. This means that you can see how impatient your ancestor was about filling in the form, or the mistakes he or she made, or how educated the writing was, which brings these people gloriously to life.

You may even find a suffragette among your forebears. In 1911, these brilliant women spoiled their census papers in protest at not having the vote. They sound like the sort of feisty females we'd have got on well with!

There is a pull from the past as we grow older, and finding out more about the relatives who went before us can be very touching. It can also give us a sense of perspective on who we really are.

WHERE TO FIND OUT MORE

Cruse Bereavement Care: www.crusebereavementcare.org.uk

Direct Gov: www.direct.gov.uk

Find My Past: www.findmypast.com

Gap Year for Grown Ups: www.gapyearforgrownups.co.uk; tel. 01892 701881

Internet Craft Fair: www.craft-fair.co.uk

Lawpack: www.lawpack.co.uk

Low Impact Living Initiative: www.lowimpact.org

The Make Lounge: www.themakelounge.com

The Man in Seat Sixty-One: www.seat61.com

National Trust: www.nationaltrust.org.uk

Next Challenges: jean@jeangaron.com; lesleypocock@aol.com

Robyn Vickers-Willis: www.navigatingmidlife.com

Stitch 'n' Bitch or Knit and Natter (http://stitchnbitch.org)

VSO: www.vso.org.uk; tel. 020 8780 7500

Women Traveling Together: www.women-traveling.com

BOOKS

Developing Resilience: A Cognitive-Behavioural Approach by Michael Neenan, published by Routledge

Mindfulness in Plain English by Bhante Henepola Gunaratana,
   published by Wisdom Publications
Navigating Midlife: Women Becoming Themselves by Robyn
   Vickers-Willis, published by Wayfinder

THAT'S ALL FOLKS . . .

So there we have it. Hopefully, we all know a bit more
now than we did on page 1 about keeping control, feeling
as fit and healthy as possible and looking great. Clearly, all
we have to do is:

1 30 minutes of exercise daily
2 Get our cholesterol down
3 Eat super-foods every day
4 Master the Mediterranean or Portfolio Diet
5 Go travelling
6 Have oodles of sex
7 See family members
8 Feed our souls
9 Meet/email friends
10 Learn new skills
11 Do facial exercises
12 . . . and pelvic floor exercises
13 Brush our skin
14 Shop for the perfect pair of black trousers
15 Do the ironing with the wrong hand to stave off
    dementia
16 Check whether our eyes are going wonky

17 Go to the dentist
18 Sort out money
19 Clear out our houses
20 Engage in altruistic activity
21 Investigate the legal position about living with friends
22 De-stress ourselves so as not to look old before our time
23 Be contemplative
24 Be happy . . .

Maybe it's not just that we're too young to get old, but that we simply won't have the time!

Index

and Psychotherapy (BACP) 39,
54
British Association for Sexual and
Relationship Therapy (BASRT)
217, 232
British Dietetic Association 101, 109,
154
British Heart Foundation 144, 145–6,
158
British Trust for Conservation
Volunteers (BTCV) 88
Brownell, Kelly 106, 107
Bucella, Marty 111
Burns, George 27
bus driving 42
businesses 19, 34, 37–42, 51, 53–4,
59, 222, 260, 281, 282–3

cab driving 41–2
calcium 102, 137
calorie reduction (CR) 155
cancer 146–53, 158
  bowel 153
  breast 148–50, 190
  of the cervix 152
  lung 152–3
  ovarian 150–1
  womb 151–2
Cancer Research UK 152, 158
car sharing 80
carbohydrates, refined 140
care homes 43, 256–7
Carer's Credit 79
Carnegie, Dale 250
cars, doing without 72, 89, 259
catalogue shopping 171–2, 177
cellulite 195, 225

charity shops 73, 170
charity work 50, 252
child minding 41, 44–5
childhood, baby boomers' 5–9, 58, 63,
  83, 87, 93, 112, 113, 160–1
children 18–19, 62–4, 98–9, 237,
  284
  and finances 58, 62–4, 72
  living with 271–2
  see also daughters
Chilton, Sally 40–1
choirs 253
cholesterol 96, 102, 115, 116, 119,
  132, 142–4
cities 258–9, 260
Citizens' Advice Bureau (CAB) 71,
  74, 80
Clark, Charles and Maureen
  The Diabetes Revolution 140, 158
classes 252, 259–60, 276, 278–9
  dance and exercise 85, 88, 89
  see also education
Classic FM 253, 254
Clear Skin UK 184, 205
Clinton, Hillary 48
clitoris 209–11
clothes 166–74
  accessories 73, 161, 167–8, 172–3
  black trousers 168
  bras 160, 164–5
  colours 173–4
  hemlines 11, 169–70
  1960s and 1970s 11, 12–13,
    160–3, 209
  opaque tights ix, 169
  and retirement 284
  selling 72

Index